FRAN
Practical Com

FRANCE
Practical Commercial Law

ALEXIS MAITLAND HUDSON
Avocat à la cour
Solicitor

LONGMAN

© Longman Group Ltd 1991

Published by
Longman Law, Tax and Finance
Longman Group UK Ltd
21–27 Lamb's Conduit Street
London WC1N 3NJ

Associated offices
Australia, Hong Kong, Malaysia, Singapore, USA

ISBN 0851 21776 1

A CIP catalogue record for this book is available from the British Library.

All rights reserved. No part of this publication may be reproduced, stored in a retrieval system, or transmitted, in any form or by any means, electronic, mechanical, photocopying, recording or otherwise, without the prior written permission of the publishers, or a licence permitting restricted copying issued by the Copyright Licensing Agency.

No responsibility for loss occasioned to any person acting or refraining from action as a result of the material in this publication can be accepted by the author or publishers.

Typeset by Servis Filmsetting Ltd, Manchester

Printed and bound in Great Britain by Biddles Ltd, Guildford, Surrey

FOREWORD AND ACKNOWLEDGMENTS

I should like to extend my thanks to Karen Delamore, Laetitia Felici, Axel Depondt and Michael Starmans whose active assistance was crucial to the writing of this book, also to Michael Soul, Jonathan Eastwood, Murray Ross and Tim Stocks for their encouragement and finally to Dr Miles Gaythwaite whose refusal to help concentrated the mind.

AMH
23 August 1991

CONTENTS

	Page
Foreword	v
Introduction	1
General	1
The Courts	3
Lawyers	5
Approach to Legal Issues	9
Do and Don't	10
Chapter One: Industrial and Intellectual Property	
1.1 Introduction	12
1.2 Patents	12
1.2.1 Procedure	12
1.2.2 Protection and Revocation	13
1.3 Trademarks	14
1.3.1 Procedure	14
1.3.2 Protection and Revocation	15
1.4 Copyright	16
1.4.1 Procedure	16
1.4.2 Protection, Exploitation and Remedies	17
1.5 Know-How, Trade Secrets and Confidential Information	19
1.5.1 Procedure	19
1.5.2 Transfer and Protection	21
1.6 Registered Designs and Models	21
1.6.1 Procedure	22
1.6.2 Use, Transfer and Protection	23
1.7 Licensing	25
1.7.1 Form and Procedure	25
Chapter Two: Competition	28
2.1 EEC Competition Law	28
2.2 The Prohibition—art 85(1)	28
2.3 The Exemptions	31
2.3.1 Block Exemptions	32
2.3.2 Opposition Procedure	36

viii   Contents

    2.3.3 Individual Exemptions   36
    2.3.4 Notification to the Commission   36
  2.4 The Consequences of Violation   37
  2.5 Article 86   38
  2.6 French Competition Law   39
    2.6.1 Articles 7–10   40
    2.6.2 Miscellaneous   42
    2.6.3 Transparency and Misleading Advertising   42
  2.7 Unfair Competition (*Concurrence dé loyale*)   43
    2.7.1 Passing Off (*imitation*)   44
    2.7.2 Unfair Advertising   44
    2.7.3 Slander of Goods and Trade Libel (*dénigrement*)   45
    2.7.4 Enticing Personnel (*débauchage*)   45
    2.7.5 Misuse of Trade Secrets   45
    2.7.6 Relief   46

Chapter Three: Business Organisations   47
  3.1 Introduction   47
  3.2 Legislation   48
  3.3 Incorporation   49
    3.3.1 Preparation of the Articles of Incorporation (*statuts*)   49
    3.3.2 The Execution of the *statuts* by all the Shareholders   50
    3.3.3 The Payment of Registration Tax (*droits d'enregistrement*)   50
    3.3.4 The opening of a *société* bank account   50
    3.3.5 Publishing a notice   50
    3.3.6 Companies Registry   50
    3.3.7 Business Formalities Centre   51
    3.3.8 *Société en Formation*   51
  3.4 Limited Liability Companies   52
    3.4.1 *Société Anonyme* (SA)   52
    3.4.2 *Société à Responsabilité Limitée*: SARL   57
  3.5 Economic Interest Group (*Groupement d'Intérêt Economique, GIE*)
     European Economic Interest Group (*Groupement Européen d'Intérêt
     Economique, GEIE*)   59
  3.6 Shareholders rights   61
    3.6.1 Access to information   61
    3.6.2 Protection of Minority Shareholders   61

Contents

3.7 Liability	62
3.7.1 Members' Liability	62
3.7.2 Company's Liability	62
3.7.3 Liability of Directors and Managers	63
3.8 Partnerships	64
3.8.1 General Partnership (*société en nom collectif* or *SNC*)	64
3.8.2 Limited Partnerships (*société en commandite simple, SCS*) Limited Partnership with share capital (*société en commandite par actions, SCA*)	65
3.8.3 Civil Company (*société civile*)	65
3.8.4 Silent partnership (*société en participation*)	66
3.9 Sole Trader (*Commerçant*)	66
3.10 Taxation Aspects	68
3.10.1 Corporation Tax (*impôt sur les sociétés*)	68
3.10.2 Personal Income Tax (*impôt sur le revenu*)	68
3.10.3 Registration Tax (*Droit d'enregistrement*)	68
3.11 Branches	69
Chapter Four: Mergers and Acquisitions	71
4.1 Mergers	71
4.1.1 Tax Treatment	75
4.2 Acquisitions	77
4.2.1 Acquisitions of Goodwill (*fonds de commerce*)	77
4.2.2 Lease of Goodwill (*Location-Gérance*)	81
4.3 Share Acquisition—Private Companies	82
4.4 Acquisition of a public company	85
4.4.1 COB	85
4.4.2 Acquisition of a *bloc de contrôle*	86
4.4.3 Take-over bids	86
4.4.4 Anti-trust provisions	87
Chapter Five: Agency	89
5.1 Background	89
5.2 Commercial Agents	89
5.2.1 Performance of the Contract	90
5.2.2 Termination of agency contracts	93
5.3 Independent Agents (*Agents d'affaire*)	94

5.4 Commission Agents (*Commissionaires*)	95
5.5 Brokers (*Courtiers*)	96
5.6 Sales Representative (*Voyageur représentant placier*)	97

Chapter Six: Distributorship — 99

6.1 Introduction	99
6.2 Exclusive Distributorship Agreements	99
6.2.1 Validity of Exclusive Distributorship Agreements	99
6.2.2 Obligations Imposed on the Grantor and on the Exclusive Distributor	101
6.3 Supply Contracts	104
6.4 Non-Exclusive Distributorship Agreements	104
6.4.1 Selective Distributorship Agreements	104
6.4.2 Approved Distributorship Agreements	105

Chapter Seven: Franchising — 106

7.1 Background	106
7.2 Franchises as licences of intellectual or industrial property	107
7.3 Franchises as Know-How Transfers	107
7.4 Control of the Franchisee's Activities	107
7.5 Exclusivity	108
7.5.1 Franchises	108
7.5.2 Pronuptia Litigation	108
7.6 Termination	108

Chapter Eight: Real Property and Succession — 109

8.1 Introduction	109
8.2 Real Property	109
8.2.1 Sale and Purchase	110
8.2.2 Business Leases	116
8.3 Succession	120

Chapter Nine: Immigration and Employment — 123

9.1 Immigration	123
9.1.1 Non-EEC Nationals	123
9.1.2 EEC Nationals	125
9.2 Employment Law Issues	125
9.2.1 Legislation	125

9.2.2 Employment Contract	126
9.2.3 Working Conditions	132
9.2.4 Worker Representation	133
9.2.5 Employee Profit Sharing Schemes	134
9.2.6 Share Options	135
9.2.7 Social Security System	135
9.3 Maternity Leave (*Congé de maternité*)	135

Chapter Ten: Taxation — 137

10.1 Introduction	137
10.2 Value Added Tax (*taxe sur la valeur ajoutée*)	137
10.3 Business Taxation	138
10.3.1 Direct Business Taxation	138
10.3.2 Tax Incentives	139
10.3.3 Indirect Business Taxation	141
10.4 Definition of Corporate Profit	142
10.5 Direct Personal Tax	143
10.6 Transfer Pricing	145

Chapter Eleven: Insolvency — 147

11.1 Introduction	147
11.2 Business Insolvency	148
11.3 Measures intended to prevent insolvency	150
11.3.1 Amber Light Proceedings (*Procédure d'alerte*)	150
11.3.2 Moratoria	150
11.4 Rehabilitation	151
11.4.1 Initiation of Proceedings	151
11.4.2 Participants in rehabilitation proceedings	152
11.4.3 The different steps in the rehabilitation proceedings	154
11.5 Rights of Creditors	159
11.5.1 Responsibilities and liabilities of the management of an insolvent business	160
11.6 Personal Insolvency	162

Chapter Twelve: Financing a French Company — 165

12.1 Introduction	165
12.2 Loans from a Bank (*contrat de prêt*)	165

12.3 Leasing (*Crédit-bail*)	167
12.4 Factoring	169
12.5 Corporate Finance	170
12.5.1 Different methods of financing a *société anonyme* (SA)	170
12.5.2 Capital Increase	172
12.5.3 Loans to other *sociétés*	172
12.6 Banking Operations	173
12.6.1 Bank Accounts	173
12.6.2 Bank Facilities	173
12.6.3 Liability of Banks and Credit Establishments	173
12.7 Negotiable Instruments	174
12.7.1 Bills of Exchange (*Lettres de change ou traites*)	174
12.7.2 Cheques	175
12.7.3 Promissory Notes	177
12.7.4 Dailly's Law	178
12.8 Guarantees	179
12.8.1 Caution	179
12.8.2 First Demand Guarantee (*Garantie à première demande*)	180
12.8.3 Guarantees by SAs	180
Chapter Thirteen: Environment and Planning	**182**
13.1 Environmental Protection	182
13.1.1 Planning Controls	182
13.1.2 Waste and Emission Control	186
13.1.3 EEC Directives	187
13.2 Planning	188
Legislation Table	191
Index	196

INTRODUCTION

General

For anyone with common law legal knowledge or training approaching French legal problems for the first time there is the obvious hurdle of coming to terms with a codified system of law in which legal precedent has a much lesser significance. In truth the divide is not so complete, since large sections of English law are now substantially codified in the form of statutes (eg The Sale of Goods Act 1979) whilst French practitioners do indeed look to the cases to clarify and expand codified legal precepts which are often startlingly lapidary in their formulation.

For the purposes of this work the principal sources of the law are:

(i)	*Code Civil*	Civil Code	CC
(ii)	*Code de Commerce*	Commercial Code	CoC
(iii)	*Code du Travail*	Employment Code	EC
(iv)	*Code Général des Impôts*	Tax Code	TC

These texts are published in separate volumes annually by two legal publishers *Dalloz* and *Litec* and incorporate any new laws which have been passed since the last edition with consequential amendments to the old texts. They are the invaluable source material to be consulted whenever the practitioner wishes to find a statement of the law. These primary sources contain numerous footnotes and references to case law which serve to illustrate the effect of any particular disposition.

For the common law lawyer the most worrying feature of dealing with a legal problem by reference to the relevant Code is the discovery that the law typically appears at first glance to be stated simplistically. As an illustration of this point Article 1382 of the Civil Code reads:

'A person who commits any wrongful act whatsoever which causes damage to another is obliged to make good that damage.'

However, there then follows many pages of footnotes and case references which seek to clarify and expand the brief statement contained in the Code. Thus at the end of the day the common law approach and the French approach are seen to produce similar results for the student or the practitioner wishing to inform himself.

Nevertheless, the French courts do not invent new remedies or restate the law and have no right to do so. It may be said that the French system in this way offers more certainty.

Amongst the most significant differences in practice between English and French law, in a commercial context, is a positive duty under the latter to execute contractual obligations in good faith. Article 1134 of the Civil Code provides:

> 'A legally binding contract must be respected by the parties to it. It may only be brought to an end by mutual consent or in a way which the law allows.
>
> It must be performed in good faith.'

It is therefore possible to reproach a party to a contract for doing or omitting to do something which is manifestly in bad faith even if it is within the scope of the contract. This example goes some way to explaining the relative brevity of French contractual documentation, since the Court has a discretion, in cases of dispute, to consider the good faith of the parties. As a result they are more prepared to accept general provisions rather than feeling obliged to be totally exhaustive and compendious.

Another significant practical difference which is crucial to doing business in France concerns the value accorded to evidence in commercial litigation. Article 109 Commercial Code provides that any means of evidence is admissible in the Commercial Court but as a matter of practice only written evidence of any fact or correspondence will have much effect. The Court fully expects the parties themselves to be less than objective in what they say and there is very seldom any oral evidence. Equally, any expert appointed unilaterally by a party will have his impartiality questioned. The Courts in general, and Commercial Courts in particular, maintain lists of court experts (*experts judiciaires*) to whom complex issues of fact, mostly technical in nature, are delegated and whose findings are generally determinative of the issues upon which their views are sought.

The involvement of court experts in disputes, frequently even before proceedings are issued, coupled with the absence of any duty to produce documents in a contentious matter analogous to the common law Discovery Procedure, should lead a non-French party to exercise considerable care in what he writes and what he expects to see confirmed in writing. French law also has a very limited notion of privilege in relation to settlement negotiations in commercial disputes. Only exchanges in writing between *avocats* marked '*confidentiel*' are privileged. Any other document may be produced in court and thus any 'without prejudice' correspondence which exists may be shown to the court by either side, often with highly prejudicial results.

As any student of comparative law knows there are more similarities than differences between most systems of substantive law. The means by which a legal result is achieved are, however, frequently diverse. As you read the chapters which follow it is the differences upon which emphasis is laid and you will need to be aware of them from the outset. The salient features of the law are covered but there is no attempt to be totally authoritative. Further research is necessary to find out all the relevant details.

THE COURTS

There are three levels of jurisdiction in the French legal system. The choice of the first level will depend both on the subject matter of the dispute, the nature of the parties and the amount in issue. Commercial disputes between commercial people (*commerçants*) as defined are always heard before the relevant Commercial Court (*tribunal de commerce*) by a lay judge. The lay judge has been elected to office from the local commercial community, either sitting alone or with two assessors in an appropriate case.

The quality of '*commerçant*' is conferred by the nature of the activity he performs and in certain cases by the holding of a specific document (*carte de commerçant*). All commercial companies both French and foreign have the necessary status to appear in the Commercial Court.

Non-commercial cases at first instance are heard by either the local inferior court (*tribunal d'instance*) or superior court (*tribunal de grande instance*) depending upon the monetary value and subject matter. The judge is a professional magistrate, but may sit with two lay assessors in an appropriate case.

Appeal from these first instance courts lies without leave to the appropriate chamber of the local Court of Appeal (*cour d'appel*). The appeal judges are professional magistrates, three of which hear any case—one presides (*président*) and the two others assist (*assesseurs*). All appeals from first instance courts are reheard *de novo* on the facts and the law.

An appeal lies from the court of appeal without leave to the appropriate section of the Supreme Court (*Cour de Cassation*) in Paris. Such an appeal may not re-open issues of fact and is on matters of law only. At least five judges hear such appeals, although in practice the hearing is often very short and there is seldom oral argument. The judges are all senior professional magistrates.

Tax causes and claims by and against the State have a separate hierarchy of tribunals (*tribunaux administratifs*) leading to ultimate appeal on legal issues to the *Conseil d'Etat*.

French courts are inquisitorial in nature. Rather than allowing the parties alone to develop their respective cases, the judge will have read the pleadings, any court expert's report (*rapport d'expertise*) and other relevant documents before the case opens and will frequently ask the parties' lawyers about them. In certain circumstances he may himself raise matters of law pertinent to the case and is bound to raise matters of public order. Oral argument is brief and frequently somewhat histrionic by English standards. Costs generally follow the event, but very seldom include a significant element in respect of lawyer's fees, although there are now signs of change in this respect.

All originating process and judgments are required to be served by a court bailiff (*huissier*) and certain other procedural matters will also be dealt with in this way.

Common law observers are inclined to think, and not without some justification, that the French legal system is based upon the premise that all litigants do not tell the truth and will seek to falsify all evidence. This is a grotesque over-simplification but it does help one to appreciate why many significant differences between (say) English and French practice and procedure exist and explains why the court mistrusts the parties' own experts, oral evidence and any proof which is not written.

LAWYERS

Dealing with any jurisdiction other than one's own is always surprising and often confusing and distressing. Problems often arise through a failure to comprehend what the foreign legal institution does or what it is designed to do. Nowhere is this more the case than when one is dealing with foreign legal professionals.

At present there is no monopoly in France over supplying legal advice or drafting legal documents. However, legislation has been introduced along the lines of German law to introduce such a monopoly. It failed initially to get a majority in the Lower House of Parliament, but was re-introduced in the Senate. This law will fuse the two existing professions of *avocat* and *conseil juridique* into a new profession of *avocat* substantially subject to the organisation and professional rules of the existing *avocat* profession with effect from 1 January 1992. It will also give to this new profession, and to notaries and certain other specific categories of French legally qualified persons, a full monopoly on the supply of legal advice and drafting of legal documents. In particular foreign lawyers, including other EEC legal professionals, would have no right to practise law, even their own, in France, unless they re-qualify locally. A special procedure has already been introduced to make this somewhat less draconian than it sounds.

At present the law in France is administered by the following professions who all have different functions, even if there is some overlap:

(i) *avocats*
 avoués
 avocats à la Cour de Cassation et au Conseil d'Etat

(ii) *notaires*
(iii) *conseils juridiques*
(iv) *greffiers*
    secrétaires-greffier
(v) *huissiers*

With the exception of *greffiers* and *secrétaires-greffiers*, legal professionals can and do practise in partnership usually as civil companies (*sociétés civiles professionnelles*) although they are rarely of similar size to their English counterparts.

If confusion is to be avoided it is necessary to consider each group in turn and what they do and do not do. A legal professional, for example, cannot be a director of a commercial company except in special circumstances which means that he may not advise the company, nor engage in any commercial activities. Indeed the practice of law is considered to be totally incompatible with any such activity:

(1) (i) The right of audience in all inferior courts, the Courts of Appeal, all administrative tribunals and criminal courts is reserved to *avocats*. However, it is not necessary to have an *avocat* in the Commercial Court and a party may nominate any person to represent him provided he is properly authorised.

(ii) Thus it can be seen that the *avocat*'s historic role is similar to that of the English barrister in relation to contentious business. His fees are negotiated directly with his client and are subject to review by the chairman of his local bar (*bâtonnier*).

(iii) The *avoué* exists only to deal with procedural matters in the Courts of Appeal and can only deal in his own district court. His involvement is compulsory and he is paid on a scale determined by the value of the case.

(iv) The *Cour de Cassation* and the *Conseil d'Etat* have a special corporation of lawyers who may alone appear in those courts and nowhere else. They deal with all aspects of such appeals and are paid a fee, usually in advance, which is freely negotiated, but usually modest in amount.

(v) *Avocats* can and do advise generally in relation to commercial matters, form companies and assist in commercial negotiations. Although the role of counsellor is increasing, it is relatively new and the number of *avocats* ready and able to perform this role is comparatively low in percentage terms. This fact alone goes a long way to explaining why there are so many foreign lawyers in Paris.

(2) (i) The essential function of the notary is to give authenticity to documents, the originals of which have been signed before him and which he conserves in his archives, delivering certified copies to those who require them. He has an official function and is considered part of the state administration and by law must be of French nationality.

(ii) Notaries have a monopoly over all real property transactions and of the proving of wills. They tend to deal with succession matters, although in France property is vested automatically in the heirs and there is no executorship function except for minors or persons under a legal disability. Notaries are allowed to act for both sides in a property transaction and have a role as arbitrator if a dispute arises in the transaction. The notary's ruling will generally be binding.

(iii) Some notaries do substantial amounts of company formation work as well as corporate and private tax advisory business. Again the numbers involved are relatively small.

(3) (i) In 1972 a law was introduced which sought to regulate the activities of unqualified lawyers

calling themselves '*conseils*' of various sorts. Thus the profession of *conseil juridique et fiscal* was born. The right to enter the profession flows from a requirement for a certain level of legal higher education either in France or abroad or membership of a foreign legal profession. A period of three years in-service training with another *conseil juridique* or *avocat* is required which can be reduced to 18 months for foreign lawyers.

(ii) The *conseil juridique* may not appear in court. There are some exceptions including the commercial court mentioned above ((1)(i)). He may engage in any other legal or paralegal work provided that he does not bring the profession into disrepute and preserves his professional independence.

(iii) The *conseil juridique* typically drafts commercial contracts, negotiates with or without his client in commercial matters and advises generally on the law and on the tax implications of various transactions. Most foreign lawyers in France, if they are locally qualified, practise as *conseils juridiques*.

(iv) Control of the profession is vested in the local state prosecutor's department (*procureur de la république*) and there are now local, regional and national groupings of *conseils juridiques* to represent the profession. Fees are freely negotiated and there is no review procedure as such. The profession will disappear by merger with the *avocats* in January 1992.

(4) The administrative function of the court is exercised by the *greffier* or *secrétaire-greffier* as the case may be. He fixes dates, sets cases down for trial, engrosses judgments and deals with the payment of court fees and all manner of general administrative matters. He does not, however,

have clients and is a salaried official of the court.
(5) (i) A *huissier*'s function is conferred by the State for a particular court. He is a ministerial official whose function is to serve documents, execute court judgments and draw up, either between the parties or unilaterally, statements of facts (*constats*) which may need to be relied upon at a later stage.
(ii) Typically the intervention of a *huissier* is required to serve notice of assignment of a debt on the debtor, to draw up the schedule of condition prior to the letting of an apartment or obtain vacant possession of a house from squatters (assisted by the local police).
(iii) The *huissier* has clients of his own and his fees in a court context are fixed by the court and for other matters are negotiated with his clients.

APPROACH TO LEGAL ISSUES

In order to negotiate contracts successfully in France or to resolve commercial disputes which may have arisen it is plainly desirable to have a feel for the legal culture which affects the thinking of your French counterpart. We have seen from the previous 'General' section that French businessmen are less pedantic in the drafting of their legal documentation and do not generally seek to provide for every fact and situation which may occur. The cost of legal proceedings in France is still generally lower than in England, not least because of the different standards of proof and absence of witnesses and oral argument in court. There is, therefore, a greater readiness to resolve matters in court if no other way can be found.

By and large the French will perform their contractual obligations in accordance with the spirit of the agreement they have made. They will not be slavishly literal-minded nor Machiavellian in their interpretation. They are, however, strongly influenced by notions the English may not have, such as the overriding duty of good faith, or the importance of the written word as a matter of proof. They are haunted by tax considerations which do not exist in the UK (for example the concept of the transfer of a '*fonds de commerce*' (see Chapter 4) is, I think, unique) and they have concerns about company law requirements which are much less developed in the UK.

As we have seen there is no requirement in French law to produce documents voluntarily to another party in civil litigation analogous to the Discovery Procedure in a common law jurisdiction. This is true also in claims by the State, although there are extensive powers of search and attachment (*perquisition et saisie*) which State entities use to overcome the problem. As a result French businessmen attach great importance to the confidential nature of documents which might be embarrassing if they were seen by others particularly the tax authorities (*fisc*). Equally an unsigned draft document has no probative value as such. French businessmen will often go to great lengths to preserve this confidentiality including depositing original documents in escrow with a lawyer for safe keeping. This seems totally foreign to the common law experience but is commonplace in France and other civil jurisdictions. You should be prepared for it and understand why it is done.

Here are some simple 'Dos' and 'Don'ts' to bear in mind when dealing with French business issues:

DO	DON'T
Write down agreed points and get both parties to sign them.	Rely on verbal assurances or your own file note.
Understand the importance of confidentiality.	Assume French law is the same as English.
Get tax advice early on in the transaction and structure it accordingly.	Get tax advice late and try to turn the deal on its head because of it.

| Research the legal background at an early stage and be assisted by your lawyer from the beginning if you need one. | Bring a lawyer into the transaction at a late stage as this will generally be seen as an unfriendly act. |

1
INDUSTRIAL AND INTELLECTUAL PROPERTY

1.1 INTRODUCTION

French law makes a distinction between industrial and intellectual property; it considers the former to be associated with trade (eg patents) and the latter to be more artistic in nature (eg copyright). The distinction is not of major significance save that there may be rights of an inchoate nature that apply to intellectual property (see below).

Although it is more extensive, in the remedies it affords in certain areas such as unfair competition, than (say) English law (see Chapter 2), French law proceeds upon basically similar lines. France is a signatory to the major international conventions on industrial and intellectual property rights, in particular the 1970 Patent Co-operation Treaty (PCT), the 1973 Munich Convention, the 1975 EEC Patent Convention, the 1975 Paris Convention on the Protection of Industrial Property (as amended) and the Geneva Convention on Copyright Protection.

1.2 PATENTS

1.2.1 PROCEDURE

The procedure by which a patent (*brevet*) is obtained in France is very similar to that in the UK and the test for novelty, inventive activity and industrial application is the same, as is the length of protection of 20 years. However, there are two protections which are different, namely:

(i) that accorded to a *certificat d'utilité* which confers rights for six years only and is useful where rapid technical advances make longer protection undesirable. The search requirements can be simplified for this protection.

(ii) that accorded to a *certificat d'addition* which relates to an improvement to an existing patent and confers protection from its own filing date to the expiry of the existing patent.

French patent applications are dealt with by the *Institut National de la Propriété Industrielle* (INPI) and those for EEC, European or PCT patents in accordance with those conventions. Filings and the grant of patents in France are published in the *Bulletin Officiel de la Propriété Industrielle* (BOPI). Equally, registrable dealings with patents such as sales and licences require registration with INPI.

There is no profession in France which has a monopoly over dealing with industrial or intellectual property analogous to the Patent Agent in the UK (before the Copyright, Designs and Patents Act of 1988 removed this monopoly). There exists a corporation of *conseils en brevets et inventions* but there is no formal training requirement, no disciplinary code and no central complaints procedure.

1.2.2 PROTECTION AND REVOCATION

A valid patent is protected by the right to claim damages for infringement, injunctions to restrain continuance and delivery up or destruction of infringing articles. The latter may be attached as a preliminary matter by a *saisie-contrefaçon* ordered by the local Superior Court (*tribunal de grande instance*) having jurisdiction over the alleged infringer. A *huissier* will prepare a list of infringing products and take custody of them pending trial. Within 15 days of the attachment substantive proceedings for infringement must start in one of the specialised Superior Courts or the attachment will be set aside and damages may be claimed by the party attached. An injunction to restrain continuance coupled with a daily fine (*astreinte*), if not observed may be ordered together with the attachment. By and large such remedies are more easily obtainable in France than their equivalents in England but the implied cross-undertaking in damages which flows from them is generally enforced if the substantive action fails.

Not only can the holder of the relevant patent sue for

infringement but an exclusive licensee may also do so. Any licensee may intervene in the proceedings or indeed, in the case of statutory licensees, bring them himself if the holder declines or neglects to after a request so to do. If the action succeeds the defendant will be ordered to pay damages equivalent to the plaintiff's lost profits from the infringement, but not conversion damages although there may be a punitive element.

A petition for revocation of a French patent may be brought before one of the specialised Superior Courts by anyone interested upon the footing that:
  (i) it should not have been granted because the invention is not patentable.
  (ii) it is insufficiently precise to enable a person skilled in the art to use it, or
  (iii) it is wider than it needs to be.

A revocation may be partial or total. There is no ground for revocation of 'obtaining' as in English law except in the case of a European patent. However, the person claiming to be the true inventor may bring proceedings (*action en revendication*) to claim the stolen patent as his own.

1.3 TRADEMARKS

1.3.1 PROCEDURE

French practice and procedure relating to what may become a trademark and to the granting of a trade or service mark is very similar to the English save that INPI, charged with dealing with trademark applications, does not itself enquire as to the distinctiveness of the mark. This is left to the parties to litigate in case of similarities. French law has a number of categories of mark of which the three most pertinent are:
  (i) trademarks;
  (ii) distribution marks;
  (iii) service marks.

The first applies only to the manufacturer of the goods, the second, however, is placed on goods by someone who distributes goods he has not made himself. A French party wishing to register may file his application with either the INPI, the local Commercial Court or Superior Court. A foreign party may only do so with the INPI and must agree at the time of registration to submit to French jurisdiction.

Once the various procedural requirements are satisfied the mark is registered in the National Register of Marks (*registre national des marques*) and published in the BOPI. In the event of rejection of the application there are specific time limits to challenge the registrar's decision. A registered mark grants protection for ten years provided that in any five year period it is actually used. It may be renewed indefinitely for successive ten year periods subject to the same proviso as to use.

1.3.2 PROTECTION AND REVOCATION

Mere use by the proprietor of an unregistered mark will not give any protection. The law only sanctions infringements of registered marks. The establishment of Goodwill in an unregistered name may confer other rights particularly in relation to unfair competition (see **2.7** below). The fact that a mark is registered will not grant any rights if a previous identical mark exists or one similar enough to cause confusion.

A valid mark, however, gives the owner the right to sue for infringement. A licensee may not do so, but may intervene in any action for damages. The test for what constitutes an infringement is not set out, but, as in England, the matter rests on the possibility of confusion in the minds of the public. The various procedures available are similar to those for patent infringement (*qv*) including *saisies-contrefaçon*, *astreinte*, temporary injunctions and delivery up or destruction of infringing articles. There are also criminal penalties including imprisonment for infringement, but they are of little practical significance.

A registered mark may be revoked if it infringes a prior mark at the suit of the prior holder or if it can be shown to have been improperly registered. Such an action is brought in the Superior Court. A mark may be lost if it is not used for five years, if it is not renewed or if the holder positively abandons it.

France is, as we have seen, a party to the Paris Convention

and also the Madrid Arrangement, so that reciprocal registration and preservation of priority is readily available.

1.4 COPYRIGHT

As befits a country which has played host to so many distinguished artists France has a well-developed law of copyright (*droit de la propriété littéraire et artistique*). It is wider ranging than its English equivalent awarding moral damages for infringement. The law also gives sculptors and painters the right to a statutory royalty of three per cent whenever one of their works is sold professionally (*droit de suite*). In a business context the relevance of this body of law is limited.

1.4.1 PROCEDURE

Copyright as a legal protection is anomalous in this chapter in that it requires no formal step to be created nor does it require publication. The protection attaches to a vast range of artistic creations, although it is the creation itself not the idea which is protected. The Law of 11 March 1957 relating to Intellectual Property ('the 1957 Law') specifies the following as being entitled to protection:
—dramatic works
—books and brochures
—literary, artistic and scientific writings
—speeches and sermons
—pleadings
—musical works
—choreographic works
—circus acts and pantomimes
(the last three having been reduced to writing in cognate notation)
—films and audiovisual works
—paintings and designs
—architectural drawings and architectural sculpture
—engravings and lithographic reproductions
—sculpture
—photographs and photographic works

—maps and illustrations
—original titles
—computer programs (Law 85.660 of 3 July 1985)

Furthermore translation, adaptations and arrangements of works already in existence are also protected.

French law makes a distinction between the rights which derive from a copyright work of a financial nature (*droits patrimoniaux*) and those which attach to its nature as an artistic creation (*droits moraux*). They are quite distinct. The first derives from the exclusive right to exploit the work for financial reward. It survives the author for fifty years after his death or seventy years in the case of a musical composition. If the work is a computer program the period is twenty-five years and runs from the date it was written. There are limited exceptions to the exclusivity referred to above principally relating to bona fide study or non-commercial family use.

The second component, the *droit moral* confers upon the author of a copyright work the right to control the way his work is exploited long after it may have been sold, or otherwise alienated. Article 6 (1) of the 1957 Law defines these rights as comprising, for the author, a right to the respect of his name, to his status as author and the integrity of his work and is similar in this respect to the moral rights created by ss 77–83 of the UK Copyright, Designs and Patents Act 1988. The moral right is inalienable, perpetual and exclusive to the author during his life and in perpetuity to his direct descendants. For a work of this nature, it is perhaps unnecessary to dwell further on this aspect save to mention that the author of a copyright work may prevent an adaptation or alteration of his work on this basis which may be significant in a commercial context.

1.4.2 PROTECTION, EXPLOITATION AND REMEDIES

The basic rule is that only the author is protected. If there has been a transfer of the right to publish or use a copyright, care must be taken to oblige the author to protect the copyright at the expense of (say) his publisher and to lend his name to any proceedings. Equally, since the damages awarded will accrue to the author, a third party with vested rights must make sure that he is entitled to them or to a proportion thereof. There are special rules which apply to compilation works with several authors and to the production of audio and audiovisual works, as well as works produced by an employee which should not concern us here.

The author may sell his patrimonial rights, his moral rights are unaffected. There are a vast range of forms of such sale from one-off performances for a fee to lump sum sales of all patrimonial rights. However, an author may not sell the whole of his further production. Such contracts are interpreted strictly and in favour of the author. There are few, if any, implied rights and the contract must be very explicit. The basic premise set out in art 35 of the 1957 Law is that an author should be remunerated periodically but the law allows lump sum sales where periodical payments would be excessively difficult or expensive to administrate or determine. A lump sum payment, however, is always possible for computer programs. There is a specific provision in art 37 of the 1957 Law which allows the author to challenge a lump sum payment if the work is much more successful than the parties thought it would be and enables the court to award a complementary sum. The original payment must have been less than five-twelfths of what would have been agreed if the actual proceeds had been known at the time of the sale. In addition to bilateral accords, France has its complement of specialised organisations which manage, license and promote the works of their members. The best known, perhaps, is SPADEM whose initials appear on the bottom of many poster reproductions of French contemporary artworks on sale in the UK.

Infringement of copyrights which consists in any form of unauthorised reproduction, production, dissemination, translation, adaptation and the like of the work is actionable and has both civil and penal sanctions. Not to respect the moral rights of the author is considered to be infringement as is 'knowingly dealing in directly or indirectly infringing goods' (Penal Code art 425 (3)).

The remedies available are broadly similar to those for patent and trademark infringement. A *saisie-contrefaçon* may be ordered by the appropriate *tribunal de grande instance*. If a performance is pending, the matter must be heard by the president of the court. The author has 30 days to commence substantive proceedings thereafter, or 15 days in the case of a computer program.

Damages may be claimed either in the civil courts or by the bringing of criminal proceedings, although in the latter case there is, as in England and Wales, a higher standard of proof required. Damages may be awarded under the head of both patrimonial and moral rights. Penal sanctions include imprisonment for up to two years and a fine between FF 6,000 and FF 120,000. These sanctions may be doubled in the case of habitual offenders. The Criminal Court in addition to awarding damages has the right to order confiscation of the profits arising from the infringement as well as the equipment used for these purposes. Such profits or property are given to the author. The court may in addition order its judgments to appear in the Press at the expense of the infringers as well as closing down premises used for the infringement either temporarily or for good.

Before leaving the subject, it is worth noting that France is a signatory of both the 1974 Berne Convention for the Protection of Literary and Artistic Works and the 1952 Universal Copyright Convention of Geneva. The French Courts will and do grant protection to foreign authors and holders of copyright and except where no legal reciprocity exists, the Law of July 1964 which deals with the application of the principal of reciprocity in relation to the protection of copyright, protects an author's moral rights.

1.5 KNOW-HOW, TRADE SECRETS AND CONFIDENTIAL INFORMATION

1.5.1 PROCEDURE

Before going on to deal with the protection the law allows for know-how, trade secrets and confidential information, it is necessary, in respect of the first two at least, to define what we mean by the terms we are using:

(1) Know-how (*savoir faire*)

French law defines this as information or practices used for business purposes whether they have been patented or not. Know-how is not necessarily totally industrial and may have other components of an administrative, financial or indeed commercial nature. However, to be protected know-how must consist of proprietary, confidential and commercial material. There may be many reasons why the owner of know-how, which could obtain the benefit of a registered patent, would not wish to pursue this course and it is possible by virtue of the procedure administered by the INPI of *Enveloppes Soleau* (see **1.6.1**) to demonstrate that the owner of the know-how was the first to discover it. This introduces an element of objective proof into any dispute that may arise subsequently in relation to such a discovery.

(2) Trade secrets (*secrets de fabrique*)

French law defines a trade secret as a process of manufacture, formula, compilation of information or the like used by a person who is carrying out commercial activities and which procures him an advantage over his competitors and which he keeps confidential. It is obvious, therefore, that a trade secret is a sub-division of know-how and the significance of this distinction is really only in the penalties which the law imposes in respect of this type of know-how.

Article 418 of the French Penal Code describes the penalties which may be imposed upon any employee, agent or director, who communicates or attempts to communicate the trade secret of a commercial undertaking to a third party. Curiously the law makes a distinction as to whether the third party is or is not a resident of France. If the third party is a foreigner or a French national resident outside France, the defendant may have imposed upon him a prison term of between two and five years and a fine between

FF 1,800 and FF 120,000. If the third party is a French national resident in France, the term of imprisonment is reduced to between three months and two years and the fine to between FF 500 and FF 8,000. These sanctions are of course in addition to those which the law prescribes in its arts 177 and 179 for those engaged in corrupt practices in the course of their employment and plainly, parting with trade secrets for reward would fall within that category. In such a case, a prison term of between one and three years and a fine of between FF 900 and FF 20,000 may be imposed.

1.5.2 TRANSFER AND PROTECTION

Know-how is treated by French law as personal rights and, therefore, it is normal to license or transfer them in a similar way to other forms of intellectual property. However, the only regulation that exists under French law to limit the freedom of the parties to contract as they will, is that which applies equally to patents when know-how is acquired or transferred by a French resident, be that a company or private individuals, to another outside France.

Indeed, the transfer or other dealing with know-how is treated for tax purposes in a very similar fashion to a licence or transfer of a registered patent.

Know-how is protected by the court either by way of an action brought by the wronged party for unfair competition (see section 2.7) or by way of a claim in tort. Equally, the improper use of know-how, in relation to any form of licensing arrangement, may be the subject of a claim for breach of contract. Damages are awarded for the loss which the owner of the know-how may have suffered but unlike copyright, there is no moral element in the know-how which the law recognises.

1.6 REGISTERED DESIGN AND MODELS

A purely aesthetic creation is not patentable as a matter of French law which has no concept of anything like a design patent. This is not to say that novel aesthetic creations or designs are unprotected. If we exclude those novel creations which are capable of being patented, and which will then have that protection, it is possible to see that the subject matter of a design registration, which is defined in art 2 of the Law of 14 July 1909 ('the 1909 Law') as

> 'a new model or design, plastic shape or industrial object which is distinct from similar objects either by reason of a distinctive and cognate configuration which makes it a novelty or by one or more external features which confer upon it a novel appearance'

has much in common with the subject matter of trademarks and copyright. Indeed a registered design may, if used as a trademark benefit from both protections at one end of the spectrum and at the other, something which could be registered as a design but which may not have the protection which is attached to copyright material.

1.6.1 PROCEDURE

As we have seen, in order to qualify for registration, the design or model must be a novelty. That novelty may consist in putting together well-known elements in a new way or can consist of something which is entirely new.

In order to be protected, the design or model must be duly registered with the INPI by or on behalf of its creator. It is possible to register the design by appointing an agent who is domiciled in France. By also registering his design or model, the creator of it establishes a presumption, which is, however, rebuttable in that it is his own original creation. However in common with trademarks, the INPI do not do any sort of search to determine the novelty or otherwise of the registered design or model and proceedings may be brought by a third party to establish rights to the design even after it has been registered.

For the designer who does not wish to go through the registration process, there is the inconvenient fact that, in case of alleged infringements, he would have to demonstrate the originality of his creation in point of time by any other means at his disposal and would have no presumption of originality. This difficulty may be attenuated by going through the *Enveloppe Soleau* procedure which has been mentioned above in section **1.4.1** and which will assist to this end. The design is put into two identical envelopes one of which is dated, stamped and sealed by INPI and returned and the other retained for future reference in case of dispute.

Registrations are made in Paris with INPI, if the creator is a foreigner or is established in Paris. Outside Paris, the designer may either register with the INPI or with the clerk of the Commercial Court in the area in which he is established. Since France is a signatory of the Paris Convention for the Protection of Industrial Property, the designer who has filed for registration may do so in other signatory countries within six months of his application and obtain the same priority as he would have in France.

The maximum period of protection accorded to a registered design or model is fifty years from the date of filing the application. However, depending on considerations of publication, it is possible to see three elements in this fifty year period. During the first five year period, the designer has the option of requesting that the design or model be put in the public domain or be maintained confidential. At any time prior to the expiration of the initial five year period the designer may apply for an extension for an additional twenty years. The option of confidentiality or disclosure remains open during this second period. A further extension of twenty years is possible if applied for before the expiration of the second twenty year period. However, in the last period there can be no maintenance of confidentiality and the design or model must be disclosed to the public.

1.6.2 USE, TRANSFER AND PROTECTION

The creator of a design or model has the right, in common with the owner of copyright, to the exclusive exploitation of it. This is of course the case whether or not it is registered and the evidential difficulties that arise in the absence of registration have been mentioned in the previous section. The 1957 Law provides in art 30 (2) that the sale of a design or model does not in itself transfer the right to reproduce it. Plainly, it is desirable then that, in any contracts dealing with transfer of rights, this point is clearly dealt with even though the relevant article of the 1957 Law does not require writing for an agreement to transfer such rights. Much in the same way as for copyright, the designer must be compensated either by periodical payments or by a lump sum and in the latter case there is a similar provision that, if the design or model is very successful, the designer may seek to have his remuneration increased. Here again, the threshold value is five-twelfths of the amount that could have been paid had the parties been aware of the financial results produced by the exploitation. Furthermore, if the beneficiary of an agreement transferring rights to such design or model is to have the right to modify or develop it in any way, he must specify this very carefully in the agreement since such a right would not be implied. There is the same obligation to notify the Ministry of Industry in relation to contracts or amendments thereto for the transfer or exploitation of designs or models where the beneficiary has his principal place of business outside France.

The remedies available to the designer or the beneficiary of an agreement relating thereto for infringement of the design or model are very similar to those others we have seen in relation to other aspects of intellectual property. There is the same option for civil or criminal proceedings although for infringements of design there is no risk of imprisonment. A *saisie-contrefaçon* may be ordered by the *tribunal de grande instance*. The damages which may be claimed in a civil suit for infringement of a design or model are to compensate the victim for the damage caused by the infringement. In addition, the court may order confiscation of the infringing production or indeed of the means of producing the infringement. The latter sanction is not available against a party who acted in good faith.

France is a party to the Hague Arrangement relating to designs and models which permits the obtaining of analogous rights in other signatory countries providing that an application is made to the International Office of Intellectual Property in Geneva and the other requirements of the Arrangement are respected.

1.7 LICENSING

The purpose of this section is to set out briefly in relation to the rights enumerated in sections **1.1** to **1.6** the features of licence agreements relating to them. Patent, know-how and trademark licences are subject to the general provisions of EEC law governing competition which are dealt with in Chapter 2. There are circulars which deal with such licences and specific regulations such as No. 2349/84 which seek to clarify the position by making certain typical clauses either acceptable or not acceptable in and of themselves in this context. However, we shall not deal further with such aspects here.

1.7.1 FORM AND PROCEDURE

All such licences, if they involve the transfer of rights to non-French nationals, are subject to reporting requirements and the royalties paid have to be declared to the Ministry of Industry each year. Failure to do so gives rise to penal sanctions as set out in art 5 of the Law of 26 December 1966.

Such a licence must be in writing and as we have seen, will normally provide for periodical payments of royalties calculated by reference to the turnover or profits of the licensee. There is no implied right to sublicense since such licences are considered to be granted '*intuiti personnae*' ie strictly personally. If such a right is required, it must be spelt out explicitly. Licence agreements relating to patents and trademarks must be registered with the INPI if they are to be effective against third parties, as must any modification thereto. Unless the licence forbids it, the owner of the rights transferred will be permitted to use them himself including within the licenced territory, if the licence is limited geographically. The owner warrants the validity of the patent or the mark but it is desirable to include the usual warranties and mutual covenants frequently found in common law style licence documentation. All rights granted in relation to licences of this type, with the possible exception of patents, are capable of being transferred by the licensee without the licensor's consent together with his Goodwill (*fonds de commerce*). Goodwill in this context is discussed below and is peculiar to the French system of analysis of business assets. If it is desired to restrict such a right of transfer then the licence should specifically exclude it. In this way the licensor has a measure of control over the character and ownership of the particular licensee he has chosen. Equally provisions may be inserted determining the licence either automatically or at the licensor's option in the case of a substantive change in the beneficial ownership of a corporate licensee.

Unless the licence excludes it the licensor has the right to sell or otherwise transfer the licensed rights subject only to an obligation to ensure quiet enjoyment of them. A licensee may wish to insert a restriction on that free transfer or sale but no such restriction will be implied. There is a presumption in the 1957 Law in respect of copyright that a periodical royalty payment will be made and French practice is weighted in favour of such arrangements. However, other language can displace the presumption and lump sum licences are sometimes granted.

In common with the position in the United Kingdom, in relation to patents there are provisions which enable a patentee to grant non-exclusive licences to anyone wishing to take one by so notifying INPI. These are called *licences de droit* and the willingness to grant them reduces the patentee's renewal fees.

Furthermore, there are, as in the United Kingdom, instances where a licence may be obtained even where the patentee will not himself grant one. These are non-consensual and arise in the case of an obligatory licence (*licence obligatoire*) by virtue of a failure to use, exploit or prepare for the use and exploitation of a patent either for three years after issue or four years after application or for a three year period during the currency of the patent. Application is made to the *tribunal de grande instance* and the order of the court will specify the terms of the licence including the royalties payable. The court may not, however, grant an exclusive licence in this way.

A similar licence known as a dependant licence (*licence de dépendance*) may be obtained by the holder of a *certificat d'addition* or improvement patent from the holder of the original patent and vice versa either after three years from issue of it or four years from the application for it, to enable the patentee to exploit his rights. Similarly the original patentee of the invention may seek such a licence from the holder of a *certificat d'addition* or improvement patent.

Finally, France has provision for the grant of licences of right (*licences d'office*) in respect of inventions, normally medical in nature, deemed necessary for public health, the national economy or defence. Depending upon the subject matter of the patent a decree is made by the relevant Minister granting the licence. This may well be exclusive, although the amount of the royalty payable is left to the local *tribunal de grande instance* of the patentee in the first case but by the Paris Court for the latter two. The State may only seek a licence for itself in the case of defence matters.

A disposal of the right to exploit intellectual property whether by sale or licence will generally be subject to value added tax as well as income or corporation tax and possibly registration tax, especially if it is associated with a sale of Goodwill. Care must, therefore, be taken to structure the licence agreement in the knowledge of what tax implications it will have in France and advice on these aspects should be sought at an early stage.

2
COMPETITION

2.1 EEC COMPETITION LAW

The Treaty of Rome is designed to create a Common Market in which goods, services, labour and capital move freely throughout the Community as they do within the national territory of each Member State. One of the conditions of reaching the Single Market is the preservation of effective competition within the Community.

The competition regulations of the EEC are based on arts 85 and 86 of the Treaty. The interpretation of these rules by the Commission and the Court of Justice of the European Community has created a body of law that is applicable throughout the Common Market and which takes precedence over national competition laws. Community law does not allow Member States to pass laws which enable businesses within their jurisdiction to act in conflict with it.

Businessmen can no longer afford to ignore EEC competition rules. An outline of the basic principles of EEC competition law is necessary in order to describe the system of French competition law.

2.2 THE PROHIBITION—ART 85 (1)

Article 85 (1) prohibits all agreements between undertakings, decisions by associations of undertakings and concerted practices which may affect trade between Member States and which have as their object or effect the prevention, restriction or distortion of competition within the Common Market.

A particular commercial activity will be caught by this prohibition if it meets the following elements:

(1) Collusion between undertakings

The term undertaking must be viewed in its broadest sense and will include an individual. There must be some economic activity, but profit-making is immaterial. The activity of an undertaking situated outside the Common Market may infringe art 85 (1), if it affects trade in the Common Market. An agreement between a parent company and a wholly-owned subsidiary will normally fall outside the prohibition. Article 85 (1) applies only to an activity between two or more undertakings. A wholly-owned subsidiary enjoys no economic independence and is therefore not a separate economic undertaking. In the case of partly-owned subsidiaries the same applies if the subsidiary has no real freedom to determine its course of action in the market.

(2) Agreements, decisions and concerted practice

An agreement will be caught by art 85 if parties reach consensus on a plan which limits their commercial freedom by determining the lines of their mutual action. No contractual terms, or written contract are required. The prohibition applies both to horizontal and vertical agreements. Horizontal agreements are made by undertakings which compete with each other since they operate at the same level of trade (for example an agreement between two manufacturers). Vertical agreements are agreements made by undertakings which are complementary to each other; they operate at different levels of the same commercial process (for example the agreement between a manufacturer and a distributor). A decision by an association of undertakings includes any decision or recommendation made in accordance with the rules of a trade association to its members, whether binding or not.

A concerted practice relates to a form of co-operation between undertakings where the undertakings involved, without having reached the stage where an agreement has been concluded, knowingly substitute practical co-operation for competition. Such a practice may be inferred if behaviour in the market is observed and close contact between the parties is proved.

(3) Trade between Member States

The fact that an agreement encourages the increase in the volume of trade between States is not sufficient to exclude its ability to affect trade between Member States. It will be affected, if it can be demonstrated that the agreement alters the normal flow or pattern of the trade or causes trade to develop differently from the way in which it would have developed in the absence of the agreement. Even an agreement made by parties located in only one Member State can infringe art 85 (1), if the agreement makes the penetration of that national market more difficult.

(4) Prevention, restriction or distortion of competition

An agreement will be prohibited under art 85 (1) if its object or effect is the prevention, restriction or distortion of competition within the Common Market. It follows that a restriction clause in an agreement can thus be caught by art 85 (1). Each agreement must be considered on its own merits. It must be decided whether the restriction is material and whether sufficient competition in the product in question still exists. Competition will not generally be impaired, if the agreement is objectively necessary for the penetration of a new area by an undertaking.

'*De minimis*' agreements will normally fall outside the prohibition of art 85 (1), because they do not have a noticeable effect on competition or trade between Member States, even if their object or effect is plainly restrictive of competition. Normally, agreements will not have a significant effect on competition where the undertaking concerned does not have a market share of more than 5 per cent in the relevant product and geographical market, and the combined turnover of the participating undertakings does not exceed 200 million ECU. Further guidance on the application of the '*de minimis*' doctrine can be obtained from the

Commission's Notice on Agreements of Minor Importance OJ (1986) C231/2.
(5) Examples of prohibited behaviour
Article 85 (1) provides a non-exclusive list of prohibited behaviour. The following arrangements are very likely to infringe art 85 (1):
  (i) price fixing agreements, including private codes of conduct on pricing and exchange of information about prices;
  (ii) restrictions on production, investment and research;
  (iii) market sharing, such as agreements to sell only in a given area (including export bans) or agreements not to operate on the partner's home market;
  (iv) application of dissimilar conditions to equivalent transactions with other trading parties, thereby making it harder for them to compete;
  (v) tie-in agreements, by imposing any obligation on customers or suppliers to buy or supply another service having no connection with the original product or service.

2.3 THE EXEMPTIONS

The general prohibition of art 85 (1) can be declared inapplicable by the Commission if the harmful effects of the restrictive agreement or practice are sufficiently counterbalanced by a number of beneficial elements. An agreement will be exempted if it fulfils the four requirements listed in art 85 (3):
—the agreement must improve the production or distribution of goods, or promote technical or economic progress;
—the agreement must allow consumers a fair share of the resulting benefit (for example in the form of lower prices or quality improvements of the goods);
—only restrictions on competition which are indispensable in order to achieve the beneficial objectives will be allowed;

—competition must not be eliminated in respect of a substantial part of the products in question.

If an agreement satisfies all four conditions, exemption may be granted under art 85 (3), either by category (block exemption) or by way of an individual decision of the Commission.

2.3.1 BLOCK EXEMPTIONS

Since the Commission grants very few individual exemptions under art 85 (3), it is advisable to consider whether a particular agreement falls within one of the block exemptions in force. If it does, it enjoys exemption unless and until the Commission makes a decision determining the exemption for the future. Where it is not possible to bring a contract within the terms of the block exemption, there is much to be said for getting it as close as possible, as the Commission has occasionally granted an individual exemption by analogy to the block exemption.

The Commission has issued several Regulations providing block exemptions for the following categories of agreement:

(1) Exclusive distribution agreements (Regulation 1983/83)

Regulation 1983/83 applies only to distribution agreements between two parties; it exempts the agreements in which the supplier agrees to deliver certain products to the distributor for resale within the whole or a defined area of the Common Market. The supplier and distributor may not be competing manufacturers of the contract goods if they enter into reciprocal exclusive distribution agreements.

The restrictions which may be imposed on the distributor include the obligation not to manufacture or distribute goods which compete with the contract goods, nor to promote sales or solicit customers actively outside the contract territory, or the obligation to purchase complete ranges or minimum quantities of contract goods only from the supplier.

(2) Exclusive purchasing agreements (Regulation 1984/83)

Regulation 1984/83 applies to agreements whereby the reseller agrees with the supplier to purchase one type of goods for resale only from that supplier or from a connected undertaking. Such agreements may not exist for more than five years.

Like the above mentioned block exemption, the agreement to be exempted must be between two undertakings only and relate to the resale of goods. Again, there is only one obligation which may be imposed on the supplier, ie the obligation not to distribute the contract goods or competing goods in the reseller's principal sales area. The obligations which may be imposed on the reseller are similar to those for the distributor under Regulation 1983/83.

The main distinction between the two Regulations is that the distributor under Regulation 1983/83 is given an exclusive area, while the reseller under Regulation 1984/83 is not.

Furthermore, it is worth mentioning that Regulation 1984/83 also contains special rules relating to agreements between oil companies and petrol stations and agreements on the supply of beer by breweries.

(3) Patent licensing agreements (Regulation 2349/84)

Exemption is granted to certain patent licensing agreements, and certain combined patent and know-how licences to which only two undertakings are party. The Regulation will not apply where know-how is the dominant element and the patents are ancillary to the exploitation of the know-how.

The Regulation gives extensive lists of clauses which are permitted and those forbidden. These are too numerous and complex for further examination in this brief outline.

(4) Exclusive distribution of motor vehicles (Regulation 123/85)

This is the first block exemption devoted entirely to one particular industry. It exempts certain categories of motor vehicle distribution and servicing agreements.

(5) Specialisation agreements (Regulation 417/85)

These are agreements whereby each party agrees to specialise in the production of certain products to the exclusion of other products which are produced by the other party. The Regulation exempts agreements for reciprocal specialisation in production by means of joint production of certain products, whether this is through a jointly-owned plant, a joint venture or a common subcontractor.

The exemption is restricted to agreements between firms with a combined turnover of not more than 500 million ECUs and a market share of under 20 per cent in the Common Market.

(6) Research and development agreements (Regulation 418/85)

The Regulation exempts agreements which are entered into between undertakings for the purpose of:

—joint research and development of products or processes and joint exploitation of the results of such research and development; or

—joint exploitation of the results of research and development of products or processes jointly carried out pursuant to prior agreement between the same parties; or

—joint research and development of products or processes excluding joint exploitation of the results.

The joint research and development work must be carried out within the framework of a programme defining its objectives and the applicable field.

The term joint exploitation includes manufacturing and licensing, but does not extend to marketing and selling. Joint exploitation is only allowed if know-how resulting from the common research and development contributes, or is likely to contribute, substantially to technical or economic progress and constitutes a decisive element for the manufacturing of the new or improved products.

(7) Franchise agreements (Regulation 4087/88)

The Regulation exempts franchise agreements concerning the distribution of goods and the supply of services. It does not include production franchises, though they might be exempted either under the Regulation on patent licensing or the know-how licensing Regulation. The exemption applies on the one hand to the territorial protection granted by the franchisor to the franchisee, and on the other to the obligation on the franchisee not to deal in goods competing with those manufactured by the franchisor or bearing its trademark. Restrictions to protect the franchisor's know-how or to maintain the common identity and reputation of the trade name or the business network are permitted.

(8) Know-how licensing agreements (Regulation 559/89)

The Regulation applies to pure know-how agreements concluded solely for the exploitation of know-how, as well as mixed know-how and patent licensing agreements that are not covered by the patent licensing Regulation. Know-how is defined as a body of non-patented technical information which is both secret and substantial. The block exemption does not apply to know-how licensing agreements concerning sales only. Any of the following restrictions are permitted.

The licensee must not:
—divulge the know-how to third parties;
—grant sub-licences;
—assign the licence; or
—exploit the know-how;

should these remain secret after the termination of the agreement.

Besides the eight block exemptions mentioned above, there are five block exemptions in the transport sector, which will not be examined in detail.

2.3.2 OPPOSITION PROCEDURE

The rules governing opposition procedure are set out in Regulation 2349/84, Regulation 417/85, Regulation 418/85, Regulation 4087/88 and Regulation 559/89.

The underlying principle of the procedure is, that even if an agreement does not fully satisfy the terms of the block exemption, it can still be exempted under the applicable Regulation. Interested parties should notify the Commission in writing seeking an exemption, from which moment the agreement will be deemed covered by the block exemption, unless the Commission opposes it and notifies the parties that any exemption would have to be on an individual basis. The Commission can only oppose this exemption within a period of six months from notification.

2.3.3 INDIVIDUAL EXEMPTIONS

If an agreement fulfils the conditions set out in art 85 (3) but does not fall within one of the block exemptions, it may nevertheless benefit from an individual exemption granted by the Commission following notification. The investigation period can take a long time and a period of two or three years between notification and the reaching of a decision is not exceptional.

Alongside the opposition procedure, the Commission has introduced the system of comfort letters to avoid delays. Comfort letters are informal letters written to the parties indicating that in the Commission's view, the agreement would benefit from exemption if it does not intend to proceed to a formal decision. Although a comfort letter does not provide the parties with the same certainty as a final decision, its stature is such that national courts would have to take account of the comfort letter. The Commission cannot change its opinion, unless there has been a material change of circumstances or it appears that the letter was written on the basis of incorrect information.

2.3.4 NOTIFICATION TO THE COMMISSION

There are three reasons why the parties to an agreement should notify the Commission:

(1) Notification is necessary for the Commission to grant negative clearance or an individual exemption. The parties can seek a negative clearance if, in their opinion, the agreement does not violate art 85 (1) at all. An individual exemption is granted if the agreement is caught by art 85 (1) but meets the conditions for exemption under art 85 (3).

(2) For the period between notification and the final or provisional decision of the Commission, no administrative fines can be imposed by the Commission.

(3) An opposition procedure under a block exemption Regulation can only operate after notifying the Commission.

It follows, that if an agreement completely fulfils the requirements of one of the block exemptions, prior notification to the Commission is not required for exemption from the prohibition of art 85 (1).

The parties should make the proper notification as soon as possible after concluding the agreement since fines may still be imposed for the period preceding notification.

Notification must be made on a prescribed form known as Form A/B issued by the Commission. In this form the parties must give detailed information about themselves and the essential features and aims of the agreement.

In France, this form can be obtained from the *Bureaux de Presse et d'Information, 288 Boulevard St Germain, 75005 Paris.*

2.4 THE CONSEQUENCES OF VIOLATION—ART 85 (2)

Where an agreement is caught by art 85 (1) and is not exempted under art 85 (3), there are two consequences:

(1) The agreement is automatically void and legally unenforceable from the moment it was made. However, art 85 (2) does not necessarily render an entire agreement void. If only certain clauses in the agreement infringe the art 85 (1) criteria and if they can be severed from the rest of the agreement, the agreement minus the

offending clauses remains valid. It is a question of national law whether the clauses can be severed. In France unless a contractual provision is essential (*determinant*) to the agreement the offending clause may be severed. It is therefore desirable in drafting the contract to specify those clauses which the parties consider to be *determinant*.

(2) The Commission can order the parties to terminate the illegal behaviour and it may impose administrative fines for breaking the rules. The fines must be paid to the Commission, not the injured parties. A claim for damages by an injured party can only be brought before national courts.

In addition, practices in breach of art 85 (1) are actionable in France at the suit of the injured parties as a tort (*délit*) based upon art 1382 Civil Code. Causal connection will have to be shown as well as financial loss flowing from the practices in question.

2.5 ARTICLE 86

Whereas art 85 deals with agreements between two or more undertakings, art 86 applies where restraint on competition arises through the abuse of market power by one or more dominant undertakings. The prohibition of art 86 applies under the following conditions:

(i) Relevant market

The question of dominance by an undertaking can only be answered after identification of the relevant geographical and product market. The geographical market is the territory in which the undertaking faces competition in respect of the practices which are alleged to be abusive. One Member State alone may constitute the relevant geographical market. The relevant product market has to be determined by applying a test of interchangeability of products. For this, one has to compare the nature of the goods, their price, their use and the conditions of supply and demand in the market.

(ii) Dominant position

A dominant position will be presumed to exist when an undertaking has a market share exceeding 40 per cent of the relevant product and geographical market. A market share between 20 and 40 per cent can imply dominance if there is a significant gap between the market share of the undertaking concerned and those of its nearest competitors. Besides the market share of a specific undertaking, it is necessary to consider various other factors indicating dominance, such as barriers to entering the market.

(iii) Abuse of a dominant position

The existence of a dominant position is not in itself prohibited. There must be some form of abuse of that position. Article 86 sets out four examples of such abuse:

—directly or indirectly imposing unfair purchase or selling prices or other unfair trading conditions;

—limiting production markets or technical developments to the prejudice of consumers;

—applying dissimilar conditions to equivalent transactions with other trading parties, thereby placing them at a competitive disadvantage;

—making the conclusion of contracts subject to acceptance by the other parties of supplementary obligations which, by their nature or according to commercial usage, have no connection with the subject contracts. Article 86 does not contain a similar exemption procedure to that in art 85 (3). A dominant company can only avoid infringement of art 86 by establishing that its acts do not go beyond normal use of its economic strength within the scope of legitimate competition.

2.6 FRENCH COMPETITION LAW

Like competition law in every other Member State of the European Community, French competition law functions to complement European competition law. The promulgation of the 1986 Ordinance was necessary to bring French law into conformity with Community law in this field. Articles 7–10 of this Ordinance give the equivalent rules as contained in arts 85 and 86 of the Treaty.

2.6.1　ARTICLES 7–10

The prohibition set out in art 7 of the 1986 Ordinance uses similar wording to art 85 of the Treaty. It prohibits any agreement or concerted practice which has as its object or effect, the prevention, restriction or distortion of competition within the market. The following types of agreement are likely to infringe art 7 of the Ordinance:

(1) restrictive agreements relating to prices, such as price fixing agreements or the exchange of specific price information;

(2) market sharing agreements, especially those dividing up the market by assigning certain territories to each party or selective distribution agreements;

(3) boycott agreements, for example, agreements requiring that parties may only deal with members of a certain trade association Article 8 of the Ordinance is the equivalent of art 86 of the Treaty. It prohibits abusive exploitation of a dominant position in the domestic market or a substantial part thereof by an undertaking or a group of undertakings. In addition to this general rule, it specifically prohibits the abuse of a client's or supplier's state of economic dependence by the undertaking or a group of undertakings, if an alternative solution does not exist. Such abuse is obvious in the four listed examples:

—a refusal to sell to a competitor;

—tying agreements;

—discriminatory sales conditions; and

—the situation where an established business relationship has been terminated because the other party refuses to submit to unjustifiable business terms.

Article 9 is similar to art 85 (2) of the Treaty; both articles declare prohibited agreements null and void. The distinction is that art 9 applies to prohibited agreements as described in both arts 7 and 8, while art 85 (2) only refers to prohibited conduct as described in art 85 (1). In practice, this difference between the two systems is not material since art 86 is directly enforceable in each Member State. This means that abusive conduct under art 86 can be declared void by national courts in France by referring to art 9.

Like art 9, art 10 of the Ordinance applies to both arts 7 and 8. It provides exemption for prohibited practices when:
(i) they result from the application of a statute or statutory regulation;
(ii) the undertakings can justify that the effect of these practices will ensure economic progress and allow consumers an equitable share of the resulting benefit, without providing the undertakings concerned with the possibility of eliminating competition in respect of a substantial part of the products in question. Furthermore, these practices may not impose restrictions which go beyond those indispensable to attain the objective of progress.

Certain types of agreement, in particular those which attempt to improve the management of small or medium-sized undertakings, may be considered to satisfy these conditions by decree issued after consultation with the Competition Council (*Conseil de la Concurrence*).

However a similar system of block exemptions, developed under European law, does not exist as such under French law. In practice French courts have the power to determine whether a specific agreement falls within one of those European block exemptions. If it does, the agreement will be exempted from the prohibition under French law, although the Commission of its own motion might still investigate the matter and could initiate proceedings of its own.

2.6.2 MISCELLANEOUS

The Competition Council is the French equivalent, for these purposes, of the European Commission. Besides its advisory role in competition issues for parliamentary commissions, the government and other public organisations, it can render decisions in connection with the application of competition rules. In particular, it can impose fines on undertakings in breach of those rules. In the case of a serious and immediate violation of the rules, interlocutory measures can be enforced in urgent circumstances. If a fraudulent violation of the rules occurs, the Competition Council may initiate a criminal prosecution. All decisions of the Competition Council may be appealed to the Court of Appeal in Paris.

Apart from this measure of supervision by the Competition Council, injured parties themselves may start criminal and civil proceedings against undertakings in breach of the competition rules.

2.6.3 TRANSPARENCY AND MISLEADING ADVERTISING

The foregoing analysis of French competition law focuses on the equivalent of arts 85 and 86 of the Treaty. Like European law, these articles cover the most important part of competition law. Besides this major regulation, the 1986 Ordinance also contains provisions which affect other areas of French competition law, such as rules on publication and communication of prices, illicit sales techniques and restrictive trade practices eg sales at loss, refusals to deal (*refus de vente*) and tying agreements. (See Chapters 5, 6 and 7).

French law, as a result of the 1986 Ordinance is a good deal tougher than its UK equivalent in relation to failure to inform customers properly of the price of goods or contractual terms. This is encapsulated in the term transparency (*transparence*) and there are strict rules governing the availability and publications of such basic information to customers and particularly consumers. There are fines ranging from FF 2,500 to 5,000 for breaches of the rules and an injured party may sue for damages if any have been suffered.

Similar rules apply to certain trade practices which have been outlawed such as, pyramid selling, selling with attached premiums and the use of 'loss-leaders' (*prix d'appel*). There are civil sanctions, by way of fines, for breaches and claims by injured parties may be made for any losses suffered. The use of loss-leaders is assimilated to the third and most worrying type of offence created in this area, that of 'misleading advertising' (*publicité mensongère*).

Any advertising which contains information, statements, claims or facts which are false or misleading or relate on a very broad basis to the product being sold, is actionable on civil or criminal grounds. The fine imposed may be very severe, up to FF 250,000 or half the cost of the advertising campaign if it cost more than FF 500,000.

Any person who has aided or abetted the offence is liable to the same sanctions and this includes any advertising agency. If the seller is a company, both the PDG and the manager responsible will be criminally liable. A prison sentence of up to two years may be imposed in addition to any fine. The judge may order a retraction of the advertisement or correction in the media and may issue interlocutory injunctions to restrain continuance of the campaign.

Damages may be claimed by third parties who have suffered loss, which includes not only competitors but also consumer groups and associations.

Thus, it can be seen that great care must be exercised in any hard selling techniques or advertising campaigns to avoid these sanctions which are quite severe.

2.7 UNFAIR COMPETITION

The subject of unfair competition (*concurrence déloyale*) is one where French law comes closest to old Anglo-Saxon systems of legal precedent. There is no statutory source of law on the subject other than art 1382 (*et seq*) of the CC. However some of the behaviour which was actionable as unfair competition has now been specifically recognised by statute and prohibited such as refusal to deal (*refus de vente*) and misleading advertising (*publicité mensongère*) (see section **2.6.7**).

France permits competition between businesses, but the Courts have consistently characterised certain types of behaviour or ways of competing as unlawful. We shall deal with the principal ones below. Some, but not all, have equivalents in English law.

2.7.1 PASSING-OFF (*imitation*)

Like its English equivalent, the French notion of passing-off is based on confusion in the mind of the reasonable purchaser between two distinct makes of goods or services. It is therefore illegal to misuse the name, products, or organisation of a competitor so as to cause confusion to the public. The misuse must be of something original and within the same geographical area. If the logo or mark is registered at INPI, the behaviour complained of, may well also constitute an infringement.

Similarly, it is unlawful to imitate the appearance of products or premises if confusion is likely to result, as well as any distinctive shape. (Cass. Civ. Comm. 519/66 Bull. CIV III 351).

French law takes the matter further, perhaps, by extending the tort to non-competing products where Goodwill is abused eg Mazda cars in France are obliged to use the word *automobile* always in conjunction with the name because of the lightbulbs of the same name. This is known as parasiting (*parasitisme*).

2.7.2 UNFAIR ADVERTISING

Misleading advertising and passing-off have already been mentioned, and both would constitute unfair advertising. It is, however, illegal in France to advertise by referring to similar products sold by competitors if the competitor's product or its price can be identified and the clientèle of the competitor is likely to be enticed away as a result (Cass. Civ. Comm. (1973) D.S.Jur. 587). It is possible to refer to an entire range of products or compare prices of identical products sold under the same conditions by various competitors (Cass. Civ. Comm. (1986) D.S. Jur 436).

2.7.3 SLANDER OF GOODS AND TRADE LIBEL (*dénigrement*)

It is illegal in France to publish false or discreditable information about the goods or services of one's competitors or about the proprietors of a business in order to attract custom.

The publication can be in writing (Cour d'Appel Paris (1977) D.S. Jur. I.R. 332) or oral or by any other means. If a third party is involved, such as a newspaper it will be jointly and severally liable. In such a case the injured party is entitled to a right of reply (*droit de réponse*). A recent case has held that publication may occur by omission such as a product falsely claimed to be the only one having certain properties. (Cass. civ. comm. (1980) Bull. Civ. IV 198).

2.7.4 ENTICING PERSONNEL (*débauchage*)

It is legal to employ staff who have previously worked for a competitor and thereby acquire indirectly the skill and knowledge they obtained in that employment. However, it is unlawful to do so if:
  (i) the employee was still under contract when the offer was made;
  (ii) the employee is still bound by a valid non-competition clause;
  (iii) the sole or main purpose of the job offer was to acquire the specific know-how; or
  (iv) the employment is of several employees such that a competitor's business is unreasonably disrupted.

The burden of proof required will often be difficult for the injured competitor to discharge in either of the latter two cases.

2.7.5 MISUSE OF TRADE SECRETS

As mentioned in some detail in section **1.4.1(b)** it is illegal to divulge or procure the divulging of trade secrets (*secrets de fabrique*) and it is not necessary to repeat the matter save to repeat that it is also a criminal offence.

2.7.6 RELIEF

As with other tort claims the plaintiff in an unfair competition action must establish that there has been:
   (i)   unfair competition;
   (ii) that damage has been caused as a result;
   (iii) the amount of the loss.

Damages will generally be assessed by reference to a loss of business during the period of the unfair competition. In addition, temporary or permanent injunctions may be ordered by the court and a trader who has been found liable might be ordered to cease doing business again for a period within the same area as the plaintiff (Cass. civ. comm. (1980) Bull. civ. IV 130).

3
BUSINESS ORGANISATIONS

3.1 INTRODUCTION

There are principally two ways of carrying on a business under French law: the first is as a sole trader (*entreprise individuelle*), the second is through a corporate body (*société*).

There is, in addition, a further form of business association, the GIE, which is peculiar to French law and will be discussed later.

The former is the smallest and simplest form of business organisation in which there is no distinction between the capital of the business and the capital of the sole trader himself. The latter is more complex—a *société* generally has a legal personality and thus there is a distinction between the business capital and the private capital of its participants. The liability of the participants for the debts of the *société*, depending on the type, may or may not be limited.

As a result corporate bodies may be divided into two categories depending on the different liability of the participants—the first corresponding approximately under English law to a limited liability company (where participants' liability is limited to the business capital) and the second corresponding more closely to an English law partnership where the members have unlimited liability for the debts of the *société*. However these divisions are much less clearly defined than they are under English law, and accordingly the form of the *société* in question should be examined separately for a clear understanding of the way in which it works.

The French system does, on the other hand, maintain a clear distinction (non-existent under English law) between commercial corporate bodies (*sociétés commerciales*) and civil corporate bodies (*sociétés civiles*). The *société* is subject to a different set of rules and a different court jurisdiction depending on whether it is considered to be *commerciale* or *civile*.

Certain forms of *sociétés* are by law *sociétés commerciales*.

Article 1 of the Law of 24 July 1966 (the equivalent to the UK Companies Act) states that

'the following forms of *société* are *sociétés commerciales*, regardless of their objects: *société anonyme, société à responsabilité limitée, société en nom collectif, société en commandite simple* and *société en commandite par actions*.

Other *sociétés* may be commercial or civil depending on their objects eg *société civile immobilière*.

Apart from the main types of *société* mentioned above, French law recognises other kinds of corporate bodies such as the *société coopérative, société à capital variable, société d'économie sociale, société immobilière pour le commerce et l'industrie* (SICOMI), but these need not detain us for the purposes of this work.

A French *société*, whether civil or commercial, is based on an agreement of a contractual nature and was originally governed exclusively by the law of contract. However the *société commerciale* has, in many respects, lost its purely contractual nature since it is subject by law to a set of mandatory rules.

Much of French company law is very similar to its English equivalent, one of the main differences being that no company may be incorporated for a term of more than 99 years. This term may be extended by special resolution on expiry of the term but never for a period exceeding 99 years.

In addition the French doctrine of *'ultra vires'* is much more limited in its extent than its English equivalent although the 1989 Companies Act has substantially reduced the gap. Similarly the need for specific authorisation of corporate action by board resolution is much reduced if the document concerned is executed by the appropriate officer of the *société*.

3.2 LEGISLATION

The three main pieces of legislation relating to French *sociétés* are:
- (i) Commercial Companies Law (*Loi sur les Sociétés Commerciales*) 66. 537 of 24 July 1966.
- (ii) Commercial Companies Decree (*Décret sur les Sociétés Commerciales*) 67.236 of 23 March 1967.

(iii) The General Companies Rules (*Dispositions Générales sur les Sociétés*) of the Civil Code book III title IX arts 1832–1844).

The first two apply only to *sociétés commerciales*; the latter applies to *sociétés civiles*, and to *sociétés commerciales* to the extent that they do not conflict with provisions of the Commercial Companies Law.

The following statutory provisions are also worth noting:

(i) Commercial Register and Companies Decree (*Décret relatif au registre du commerce et des sociétés*) 67.327 of 23 March 1967.

(ii) Economic Co-operation Group Decree (*Décret relatif au Groupement d'intérêt Economique*) 67.821 of 23 September 1967.

(iii) French accounting principles as set forth in the Law of 30 April 1983 (individual companies' financial statements), the Law of 3 January 1985 (consolidated financial statements) and finally the Rules governing the Stock Exchange Commission (*Commission des Opérations de Bourse*, known as the COB) Ordonnance 67 833 of 28 September 1967.

3.3 INCORPORATION

Setting up a French *société* involves a lengthier process than setting up an English company especially in view of the availability in England of ready made 'off-the-shelf' companies which do not exist in France. One should generally count on a period of three months. The following is a list of the principal steps to be followed in order to set up the *société* (these may differ slightly according to the nature or type of *société*):

3.3.1 PREPARATION OF THE ARTICLES OF INCORPORATION (*statuts*)

French law states that the *statuts* must contain, as a minimum requirement, the following information relating to the *société*:

(i) its object;
(ii) its name (a name search should be carried out as a

preliminary step at INPI, *Institut National de la Propriété Industrielle*) to make sure the name is available;
(iii) its registered office;
(iv) its duration;
(v) declaration of its legal form;
(vi) the amount of its registered capital (if any);
(vii) the type and number of its shares.

In all other respects the shareholders may, in theory, include any other provisions they wish. In practice the *statuts* often consist mainly of standard provisions which are similar to their English counterparts. However there is no equivalent of the standard English *Table A* Articles.

3.3.2 THE EXECUTION OF THE *STATUTS* BY ALL THE SHAREHOLDERS

In the case of an SA (which corresponds roughly to an English Plc) these must be approved at the first general meeting.

3.3.3 THE PAYMENT OF REGISTRATION TAX (*droits d'enregistrement*)

And the subsequent stamping of the document.

3.3.4 THE OPENING OF A *SOCIÉTÉ* BANK ACCOUNT

The depositing of the minimum share capital required for the particular form of 'société' in question, in return for which the bank issues a certificate (*certificat de dépôt*).

3.3.5 PUBLISHING A NOTICE

The publishing of a notice announcing the incorporation of the *société* in a legal gazette.

3.3.6 COMPANIES REGISTRY

In the case of civil companies the filing with the clerk of the *société*'s local Companies Registry (*tribunal de commerce*) of the following documents:

Incorporation

(i) copies of the *statuts*;
(ii) details of the manager (*gérant*) or directors (*administrateurs*);
(iii) copies of a subscription certificate listing the subscribers to the *société*;
(iv) copies of the report of any expert valuer (*commissaire aux apports*) valuing any contributions in kind which have been made to share capital;
(v) a declaration of conformity (*déclaration de conformité*) certifying that the proper steps have been taken in conformity with the relevant law.

3.3.7 BUSINESS FORMALITIES CENTRE

Since 1985, all registration applications for *société commerciales* are made directly to a Business Formalities Centre (*centre de formalités des entreprises*) which have been set up in most *départements*. The centre is responsible for transmitting information concerning the *société* to the appropriate government authorities including the *greffe* of the *société's* local *tribunal de commerce* who is in turn responsible for the publishing of an announcement in the *Bulletin Official des Annonces Civiles et Commerciales* (BODACC—a legal publication similar to the Official Gazette). Accordingly in the case of a *société commerciale* the documents referred to in section **3.3.6** are sent directly to the Business Formalities Centre.

3.3.8 *SOCIÉTÉ EN FORMATION*

A company does not acquire full legal status until it is registered at the appropriate Register of Commerce. Nevertheless it is able to enter into contracts whilst still *en formation* ie during the period between the signature of the *statuts* and registration, subject to subsequent ratification of the contract once the company is registered. It is possible to insert a provision in the *statuts* whereby named obligations to be assumed by the *société en formation* are automatically ratified by the *société* on its registration.

Any person acting on behalf of a *société en formation* will be held personally liable for any obligations which are assumed during this period and which are not subsequently ratified by the *société*.

A sole trader needs only to be registered at the appropriate Register of Commerce.

A non-EEC national, carrying on business in France either as a sole trader or as a manager or director of a *société*, will need to acquire a foreigner's trading card (*carte de commerçant étranger*) beforehand and fulfil the necessary requirements.

3.4 LIMITED LIABILITY COMPANIES

3.4.1 PUBLIC LIMITED COMPANY (*societe anonyme (SA)*)

(1) An SA is similar to an English Plc in its structure and purpose. It is the only form of company other than an SCA which may offer its shares to the public. It is often considered to be more suitable to large-scale operations in view of its management and control structure.

An SA has a minimum of seven shareholders, either individuals or legal entities, which may be either French or foreign. A transfer of shares (*actions*) in an SA operates either by execution of a stock transfer form (*ordre de mouvement*), in the case of registered shares, or by physical delivery, in the case of bearer shares. Since 1 October 1982, only corporations listed on a stock exchange may issue or maintain bearer shares and these must be held by authorised depositaries such as banks.

Like an English Plc, an SA may obtain finance by various different means including share issues (ordinary, redeemable and preference shares), debentures and share warrant issues and the like.

An SA must, by law, appoint at least one (and, in the case of an SA obliged to prepare consolidated accounts, two) independent statutory auditor (*commissaire aux comptes*) for a period of six years.

The main difference between the role of an English statutory auditor and that of its French counterpart is that in France a statutory auditor has not only a duty to verify that the accounts of the *société* in question have been drawn up in accordance with the law but also a duty to report to the public prosecutor any mismanagement of the company of a criminal or quasicriminal nature. Failure to do so may involve civil and criminal charges being brought against the auditor. Equally, whenever a statutory auditor is appointed, a potential substitute (*suppléant*) must also be named, in case the appointee retires during the six year period or is dismissed. This may be on the grounds of serious misconduct. Such a mechanism helps to preserve the independence of the statutory auditor by reducing the scope for applying undue pressure on him.

The passing of a resolution at an annual general meeting of the shareholders requires a simple majority. If major decisions have to be made, concerning, for instance, a merger or a change in the articles, an extraordinary shareholders' meeting must be convened and an enhanced majority of two-thirds must be obtained to pass any resolution relating thereto. Provisions governing the convening of meetings are strictly applied and consents to short notice or waivers to proper notice are extremely rare.

(2) *Capital*

A private SA must have a minimum share capital of FF 250,000 whilst a publicly quoted SA must have a minimum share capital of FF 1,500,000. French company law makes no distinction between *authorised* and *issued* capital. However a quarter of the registered capital of an SA, eg a minimum amount of FF 62,500 for a private SA, must be paid up at the date of incorporation. The unpaid balance is a debt due by the shareholders to the SA and can be called up at any time.

All shares must have a nominal value which is fixed by the *statuts*. Since 1988, there is no minimum nominal value requirement except in the case of a publicly-quoted company whose shares must have a nominal value of at least FF 10 expressed in francs excluding centimes.

A quoted SA must obtain the prior approval (*visa*) of the COB for a share issue by filing an information report (*note d'information*) (see Chapter 4). It is possible to transform an SA into a SARL or a *société en nom collectif* or SNC in certain circumstances, but it is rare.

(3) *Management of SA*

There are two forms of management structure, the most usual form, the single-tier system, consists of a board of directors (*conseil d'administration*) and a chairman (*Président Directeur Général* or PDG), the other, the two-tier system (adopted by the Law of 24 July 1966) consists of a directorate (*directoire*) and a supervisory board (*conseil de surveillance*). The latter system, which is based on the German model, is rare in practice except in major Plcs with a substantial workforce, where union representatives will often sit on the supervisory board.

(4) *One-Tier System*
   (i) Board of Directors (*conseil d'administration*)

The board of directors must have a minimum of three and a maximum of 12 members or 15 if the SA is quoted. A director may be a legal entity represented by an individual but *must* be a shareholder of the SA. The requirement for a director to hold shares in the SA is considered to both guarantee the directors' performance and to ensure his attendance at shareholders' meetings. However, no individual may be a director of more than eight SAs having their registered office in metropolitan France. There are limits on the age of board members which should be set out in the *statuts*.

As in an English company the board of directors of an SA exercises the management powers of the SA. Thus specific matters are, by statute, reserved solely to the board of directors such as the calling of shareholders' meetings, the preparation, review and adoption of budgets and accounts, the preparation of the report on the activities of the company for each fiscal year, the prior approval of certain contracts entered into between the SA and its management (and defined by art 101 of the Law of 24 July 1966) the appointment and dismissal of the PDG and general managers (*directeurs généraux*, DGs) and the allocation of directors' fees.

A director is appointed either by the *statuts* or by the SA in general meeting. He is likewise removed by the SA in general meeting.

(ii) The Chairman and Chief Executive (*Président Directeur Général*, PDG)

A PDG must be an individual chosen by the board from among its members. No individual can be PDG of more than two SAs having their registered office in metropolitan France, except in special circumstances, the most important exception being in the case of group companies.

A PDG may be assisted by up to five DGs who may be, but do not have to be, shareholders of the company. Their remuneration is treated as salary and as a result attracts favourable tax treatment as well as being deductible from company profits. Both the PDG and the DG are covered by the relevant employment legislation relating to employees (*salariés*).

(5) *Two-Tier System*

The two-tier system separates the performing of

management functions (the directorate) from the control of management (supervisory board).

(i) The Directorate

The maximum number of directorate members is five (or seven if the SA is publicly quoted). Members of the directorate are appointed by the supervisory board. They may or may not be shareholders of the SA as well as employees but may only be dismissed by the shareholders in general meeting on the proposal of the supervisory board.

Members of the directorate have the same income tax status as the PDG and the DG of the one-tier system.

(ii) The Supervisory Board

A supervisory board consists of three to 12 members, which may be either representatives of legal entities or individuals whose remuneration is fixed by the SA in general meeting. A member of the supervisory board may not be an employee of the company and must be a shareholder in the SA. Members are appointed either by the *statuts* or by the SA in general meeting.

The functions of the supervisory board are mainly confined, in practice, to appointing the members of the directorate and to supervising the management of the SA.

The danger inherent in this kind of system is that a clash between the supervisory board and the directorate may create obstacles to the smooth and efficient management of the company. On the other hand, the two-tier system may offer investors the possibility of maintaining a supervisory control in the company without exposing themselves to liability under the relevant insolvency law provisions applicable to directors.

3.4.2 SOCIÉTÉ A RESPONSABILITÉ LIMITÉE: *SARL*

(1) A SARL corresponds more closely to the English private limited company (and an SA) in that its members are liable to contribute towards its debts and obligations only to the extent of their shares in the company. It is the simplest and most popular form of *société* and is extensively used by businessmen who know each other and who wish to use a limited liability vehicle without using the more complex form of SA, in the context of small to medium size operations.

The SARL must have a minimum of two and a maximum of 50 members (*associés*) either individuals or legal entities, French or foreign.

Under the law 85.69 of 7 July 1985 a SARL may be subscribed to and may continue to exist with only one shareholder. The shareholder in such a case may be an individual or a legal entity. He is known as sole member (*associé unique*). Such a SARL is known as an *Entreprise Unipersonnelle à Responsabilité Limitée* or *EURL* and is subject to the same provisions as those governing a SARL. If the sole member is an individual he may not be the sole member of another *EURL*. If the sole shareholder is a legal entity, it may not itself be a *EURL*.

Like an SA, the members of a SARL are not normally personally liable for company debts and most decisions can be made by a majority of shareholders. However it also resembles a partnership in that the personal element to its membership is important and its shares are divided into non-negotiable shares (*parts sociales*). *Parts sociales* are freely transferable among members, however, transfers to third parties are subject to the prior approval of a majority of members representing at least three-quarters of its capital. The articles may require unanimity in the case of new members. The distinction between *actions* and *parts sociales* is also important for tax purposes. A SARL may not issue negotiable bonds.

A statutory auditor is required when any two of the following conditions are satisfied concurrently:
— if the total assets of the SARL reach FF 10,000,000;
— if its total turnover or its pre-tax revenue tax reaches FF 20,000,000;
— if it has at least 50 employees.

The decision making process is somewhat simpler than that of an SA. The members in general meeting pass resolutions relating to all matters, unless the articles provide otherwise. Written resolutions are permitted if the articles so allow, except in respect of the annual approval of the accounts.

Extraordinary general meetings of the members are held from time to time to amend the articles of the SARL or to approve transfers of shares to third parties with the required majority (usually three-quarters). An annual meeting must be held within six months of the end of the financial year to approve the accounts.

It is possible to transform a SARL into an SA after at least two tax years have elapsed and the accounts in respect of those two years have been formally approved.

(2) Capital of a SARL

The minimum share capital required for the incorporation of a SARL is FF 50,000 and must, unlike in the case of an SA, be fully paid-up at the time of incorporation. Indeed, it must be paid into the bank account of the *société en formation* and the *certificat de dépôt* obtained. This certificate will be required when completing the formalities of incorporation. See section **3.3** above.

(3) Management of a SARL

A SARL is managed by one or more managers (*gérants*) who need not be members. The *gérant* has unlimited powers at law to bind the SARL both in respect of third parties and, unless these are limited by the *statuts*, in relation to the members.

There is no restriction on the number of posts of *gérant* an individual may hold.

A *gérant* who is not a member and holds less than 50 per cent of the shares in the SARL is considered as an employee. A manager who is a member and holds more than 50 per cent of the shares in the SARL is considered to be self-employed. As a result his remuneration is not a deductible expense from the profits of the company.

3.5 ECONOMIC INTEREST GROUP (*Groupement d'Intérêt Economique, GIE*) EUROPEAN ECONOMIC INTEREST GROUP (*Groupement Européen d'Intérêt Economique, GEIE*)

(1) GIE

The French GIE was created by Ordonnance No. 67-821 of 23 September 1967. It is neither, strictly speaking, a corporate body nor a partnership. It is an entity created for the purposes of a group of businesses which pool their resources to carry on some joint activity whilst maintaining their independence.

A GIE's object must be an extension of its members' ordinary business activities.

A GIE is a separate legal entity to that of its members and can be set up with or without share capital. A GIE can and does contract directly. Members are jointly and severally liable for its debts after certain procedures have been exhausted. It is fiscally transparent.

Although established principally to allow the members to pool resources to save costs, the GIE may at times realise profits or losses. Such profits or losses are attributable directly to the members which are included, in the case of corporate members, in their own P & L account. This makes the GIE a very useful tool for tax-driven financing of high value assets.

The GIE is formed by executing a written agreement between the members and incorporated by entry in the commercial register. However, a GIE may be civil or commercial depending on its purpose. (See section 3.1 above).

A GIE is a useful type of vehicle for businesses wishing to engage jointly in activities such as technological research, market studies, advertising, joint purchasing, selling, exporting or importing and the like. It offers an interesting and flexible type of association for businesses which cannot or are not willing to undertake a merger.

(2) GEIE

The GEIE was created on 25 July 1985 by Regulation 2137/85 of the EEC Council of Ministers which defines its basic characteristics and contains the rules for forming and operating a GEIE. The GEIE is a legal entity inspired by the GIE, which is designed to facilitate co-operation between businesses in different Member States of the EEC.

Membership is open to community persons, including individuals, partnerships and companies. Like the GIE, a GEIE may be formed for a wide variety of joint activities, such as research, manufacture or distribution; or could be used as a joint venture vehicle.

Since the EEC Regulation was inspired by French law relating to GIEs, the rules applicable to GEIEs are very similar to those applicable to GIEs. Specific provisions for GEIEs established in France are contained in the Law 89/377 of 13 June 1989. By virtue of this law the GEIEs acquire legal personality as soon as they have been registered in France on the commercial register. Unlike a GIE, a GEIE may not issue debentures.

3.6 SHAREHOLDERS' RIGHTS

3.6.1 ACCESS TO INFORMATION

Each shareholder has the following rights to be kept informed about his company:
  (i) a continuing right to obtain at any time information relating to the operations of the company during the past three fiscal years;
  (ii) the right to receive or to consult corporate documents in connection with the meetings of the shareholders;
  (iii) the right to receive certain periodical financial information.

3.6.2 PROTECTION OF MINORITY SHAREHOLDERS

(1) Legal protection
  (i) SA

   One or more shareholders holding at least ten per cent of the share capital of the company may, by petitioning the Commercial Court, appoint an expert to prepare a report on one or more aspects of the management of the company. This report has to be published but unlike under English law, the court has no power to take action *ex officio* if it appears that there has been mismanagement. There are similar provisions allowing one or more shareholders to submit, no more than twice a year, written questions to the PDG or president of the *directoire* concerning any matter which may materially affect the business of the company.

  (ii) SARL

   Members of an SARL may seek the appointment of an expert in the same way as a minority shareholder in an SA.

(2) Additional protection based on case law

In addition to the abovementioned rights, following a decision of the Supreme Court (*Cour de Cassation*), any shareholder may petition the competent Commercial Court for the appointment of a special administrator (*administrateur provisoire*) when exceptional circumstances prevent the normal functioning of the company or its management. Equally, the general civil law principle sanctioning the abuse of legal rights (*abus de droit*) will be applied by the court when a decision taken by the majority is against the general interests of the company or is motivated solely by an intention to favour the members of the majority to the detriment of the minority. The latter is similar to the English doctrine of fraud on a minority.

3.7 LIABILITY

3.7.1 MEMBERS' LIABILITY

The liability of members of a *société de capitaux* (SA or SARL) is generally limited to their investment in the capital of the *société*. Such limited liability also applies to certain limited partners (*commanditaires*) of a limited partnership (*société en commandite*). However, the partners of general partnerships (*société de personnes*) and GIEs are jointly and severally liable without limit for the debts of the partnership or GIE. In the case of a civil company, however, members are liable to third parties in the same proportion as their shares in the company but again without limit.

3.7.2 COMPANY'S LIABILITY

(1) Civil liability

French law protects third parties against *ultra vires* acts committed by directors or managers. The company will be bound by such acts and the burden of proof will be upon the company to avoid liability. In the absence of fraud or complicity of the injured party this burden will be difficult to discharge. In other respects the civil liability of companies or partnerships is based upon similar rules relating to breach of contract or duty, save that the relevant provision will be found in the Civil Code or Commercial Code. Remember, however, the importance of writing and the absence of oral evidence in court. Equally, France has no developed doctrine of promissory estoppel; so mere silence is generally insufficient to authorise any action or disentitle a party to rely on a defence which would otherwise be available. Part performance of an obligation which is otherwise imperfectly recorded in writing may be relied upon if it is sufficiently unequivocal.

(2) Criminal liability

Under French criminal law a company cannot itself have criminal liability. However, in certain circumstances, principally matters concerning revenue, competition and employment law, a company may be criminally liable but can only be punished by way of a fine, but see section **3.7.3** below.

3.7.3 LIABILITY OF DIRECTORS AND MANAGERS

Managers and Directors are subject to civil liability and criminal penalties for violation of the provisions of either the law or the articles and for acts of mismanagement.

This liability also attaches to a person who is not formally in a management position but who actively manages or has actively managed the company (*dirigeant de fait*) in a similar way to a shadow director under the new Insolvency Act. It is generally easier in France to pursue a negligent director or *gérant* than in the United Kingdom particularly in the case of insolvency of the company. Equally, and this must be the point of concern, if a criminal act is committed by the company it will generally be the PDG, or *gérant* as the case may be, who answers to charges in court and may be imprisoned. As in England, in France commercial insurers will not pay claims arising out of criminal liability.

3.8 PARTNERSHIPS

French law recognises general partnerships (*société en nom collectif*) and limited partnerships (*société en commandite simple*). French law also recognises the latter when they have a share capital (*société en commandite par actions* or SCA). In addition to these forms, French law also recognises civil partnerships governed by civil law (*sociétés civiles*) and silent partnerships (*sociétés en participation*). The latter is the only form of company that does not have a distinct legal personality. Its existence is generally inferred by conduct. In certain very limited cases, French law denies legal personality to partnerships which would otherwise be *sociétés* but for the status of their members. This is currently the case with partnerships of solicitors which are designated *sociétés de fait*, where they could become *sociétés civiles professionnelles* if the members were registered as *conseils juridiques* or *avocats*.

3.8.1 GENERAL PARTNERSHIP (*Société en nom collectif* or *SNC*)

This form of business association is similar to a general partnership in England. It is mainly used in France for family businesses but foreign investors may find it convenient for joint ventures if they wish to transmit profits and losses abroad for tax purposes. Unlike an English partnership, the *société en nom collectif* has a legal personality. Registration is very simple, no minimum capital is required and no minimum par value of shares is stipulated. The time and manner of paying up the capital may also be freely agreed upon among the members.

An SNC is a close body where the transfer of shares to a third party is subject to the unanimous prior approval of its members. All members have the status of *commerçants* and are jointly and severally liable for partnership debts without limit. An SNC is managed by one or more *gérants* who need not be members. Members of an SNC cannot be employees for income tax or employment protection purposes.

3.8.2 LIMITED PARTNERSHIPS (*Société en commandite simple, SCS*) LIMITED PARTNERSHIP WITH SHARE CAPITAL (*Société en commandite par actions, SCA*)

These two forms of companies are rarely used but some large French companies such as Michelin, Yves Saint Laurent and Casino have chosen to be SCAs. An SCA can offer its shares to the public. In both cases, as with an English Limited Partnership, there are separate categories of members with different status and liability:

(i) The *commandités* (general partners) have unlimited personal liability and manage the company. *Commandités* have similar powers to those of the partners in an English partnership.

(ii) The *commanditaires* (limited partners) have limited personal liability and may never take part in the management of the company. However, the *commanditaires* have the right to supervise the company's affairs in a similar way to the supervisory board of the SA. In an SCA *commanditaires* are at the same time shareholders and are represented by a supervisory board which has similar powers to those of a statutory auditor.

This sharp distinction between those who have management responsibility, similar to partners, and those who participate in the company, as investors, act as a protection against hostile takeovers.

3.8.3 CIVIL COMPANY (*Société civile*)

A civil company (*société civile*) is a company created in order to permit its members to carry out a profit-making activity which is civil by nature within a very flexible structure. *Société civiles* are frequently used as business entities for activities such as:

(i) real estate transactions involving either the purchase of land with a view to its resale after its development or renting property;

(ii) agricultural activities involving agricultural produce and the subsequent transformation and/or sale thereof; or
(iii) the exercise of a profession by, for example, lawyers, accountants, doctors and architects.

Unlike the other partnerships mentioned, a civil partnership is governed solely by the Civil Code.

A *société civile* may exist in many forms but general principles apply to all of them. Unlike an SA or a SARL, there is normally no minimum registered capital fixed by statute. The capital is divided into non-negotiable shares (*parts*) and unlike an SA or a SARL, there is no minimum par value fixed by statute.

The transfer of *parts* in a civil company must be made by a written contract of sale and duly registered with the tax authorities and requires the unanimous prior consent of all members.

All decisions of the members of a civil company, including a resolution to amend the articles, may be made at a meeting of the members upon such majority vote as is specified in the articles. If, however, the articles do not specify the majority required to adopt a resolution, resolutions may only be adopted by the unanimous vote of the members.

3.8.4 SILENT PARTNERSHIP (*Société en participation*)

This form of business association is often chosen by businesses wishing to engage jointly in a specific activity for a limited period of time. It is the only form of company that does not have a distinct legal personality and does not need to be registered.

The *société en participation* does not have a capital and may not itself be declared insolvent. Members remain individually liable for their acts. Since 1978, a *société en participation* can be secret or disclosed to third parties. Where its purpose is commercial, similar provisions apply *mutatis mutandis* as if it were a *société en nom collectif*.

3.9 SOLE TRADER (*Commerçant*)

The status of sole trader is subject to certain conditions and is incompatible with certain professions eg *avocats*.

Sole Trader (Commerçant)

Nationals of EEC Member States who wish to engage in commercial activities in France as sole traders do not need to obtain a businessman's card (*carte de commerçant*). However, any trader seeking to carry on certain regulated business or activities must obtain specialised permits or licences in the same way as a national.

Finally, upon commencing commercial activities, each trader must carry out certain formalities such as:

(i) registering with the Register of Commerce and Companies of the area in which he is to carry on his commercial activities;
(ii) registering with the competent tax authorities;
(iii) keeping complete and accurate accounting records;
(iv) taking out appropriate social security/retirement insurance.

A sole trader is personally liable for all debts arising in connection with his business. Even though a trader normally conducts his activities in his own name (*entreprise individuelle*) without creating a separate legal entity, his business operation constitutes Goodwill (*fonds de commerce*).

Goodwill refers to a group of tangible and intangible assets used by an individual or a legal entity in the conduct of a specific commercial activity. Goodwill usually includes existing and potential clientèle and those assets used to maintain and develop the clientèle such as equipment, machinery, stock, goods, leaseholds, industrial and intellectual property rights, as well as certain permits and licences for the performance of regulated activities.

Goodwill is a very important legal notion in the French business environment not only in connection with corporate reorganisations involving the sale and lease (*location-gérance*) of businesses but also in connection with the ability of the companies involved therein to obtain finance. Companies, and individuals, often pledge Goodwill as a means of giving security for loans granted to them by bank or trade creditors. Such pledges are easily registered at the Register of Commerce and Companies and once registered are effective against third parties.

Specific legislation relating to the operation, transfer, lease and pledge of Goodwill raises complex substantive legal and tax issues which require careful consideration (see section **4.2.1**).

3.10 TAXATION ASPECTS

3.10.1 CORPORATION TAX (*Impôt sur les sociétés*)

The rate of corporation tax was 50 per cent in 1988, 42 per cent in 1989 and 37 per cent in 1990 on undistributed profits (34 per cent is expected for 1991).

The corporation tax was fifty per cent in 1988, 42 per cent in 1989 and 42 per cent in 1990 on distributed profits (37 per cent is expected for 1991).

Companies subject to corporation tax are listed in art 206.1 of the French TC such as *sociétés anonymes, sociétés à responsabilité limitée, sociétés en commandite par actions, sociétés coopératives*.

3.10.2 PERSONAL INCOME TAX (*Impôt sur le revenu*)

Sole traders or members of companies which are not subject to corporation tax are normally subject to personal income tax (up to 56.8 per cent for an income over FF 493,540) and if they are a corporate entity they are subject to corporation tax on their share of profits.

However, the following companies may elect to be subject to corporation tax: *sociétés en nom collectif, sociétés en commandite simple*, a commercial *société en participation*, but such an option, once exercised, is irrevocable.

3.10.3 REGISTRATION TAX (*Droit d'enregistrement*)

Share transactions other than those involving transfers of *actions* in an SA are subject to a registration tax of 4.8 per cent.

Actions in an SA are not normally subject to registration tax unless such a transfer is contained in a written agreement and the transfer is followed by a change of purpose. If so contained there is now a flat rate *ad valorem* duty of 1 per cent. This duty is, however, territorial and if the agreement is signed bona fide outside France it is avoided. A transfer by simple stock transfer (*ordre de mouvement*) is not stampable.

Contributions in kind to a company such as real estate or goodwill are subject to registration tax.

The law provides for the application of two different rates, depending on the circumstances:

(i) One per cent of the value of the contribution, if it is effected by an individual for the benefit of a company which is not subject to corporation tax.

(ii) One per cent of the value of the contribution, if it is effected by a company which is subject to corporation tax for the benefit of a similarly taxed company.

(iii) 11.40 per cent of the value of the contribution, if it is effected by an individual or by a company not subject to corporation tax for the benefit of a company which is so subject or vice versa.

3.11 BRANCHES

Branches (*succursales*) are preferred by some foreign investors because of the less onerous legal and formal requirements they entail such as simple management, no minimum capital, no articles of incorporation.

Some investors also feel that the procedures involved in setting up a branch are simpler. In practice, however, it is neither simpler nor quicker to form a branch than to set up a limited liability company or some form of partnership.

Most formalities are the same, the basic difference being that for a branch, the articles of association of the foreign corporation must be translated into French, whereas a French company must draw up its own articles in accordance with French company law requirements. In addition a direct investment declaration (*déclaration d'investissement direct*) must be made to the French Treasury (*Ministère de l'Economie, Direction du Trésor*). The manager of a branch who is not an EEC national must hold a *carte de commerçant étranger*.

Another reason the branch form may be preferred lies in the possibility of obtaining corporate tax relief at home when a new investment is expected to generate losses in its initial years.

However, branches present a number of major drawbacks. One of the most important of these is the fact that the foreign head office is liable for debts incurred, which means that head office records are not privileged from investigation by the French tax authorities should the branch's financial statements appear worthy of investigation. In practice, branches are often used in the banking sector to minimise the cost of borrowed funds and to test the waters prior to the establishment of a French subsidiary of whatever form is actually chosen at the end of the day. The losses realised in the early years may be relieved in the home country, but care needs to be exercised when establishing a subsidiary subsequently to avoid adverse tax implications such as the transfer of Goodwill which, as we will see, may be taxed at up to 14.2 per cent.

4
MERGERS AND ACQUISITIONS

4.1 MERGERS

There are three forms of corporate re-organisations commonly practised in France—these are: merger (*fusion*), hive-off (*scission*) and partial asset transfer (*apport partiel d'actif*).

The provisions governing mergers and hive-offs are to be found in arts L371–389 of the Law of 24 July 1966 (as amended by the Law of 5 January 1988) and arts D 245–265 of the Decree of 23 March 1967 (as amended by Decree n° 88-418 of 22 April 1988) the later provisions being designed to keep French law in this area consistent with the relevant EEC directives.

A merger is a transaction whereby one or more companies may transfer their undertaking to an existing company (*fusion-absorption*) or newly formed company (*fusion-réunion*). The most common form of merger practised in France is the *fusion-absorption* an alternative which does not currently exist under English law. It is usual for the larger company to absorb the smaller.

A hive-off is 'a transaction whereby the undertaking of one company is divided and transferred to two or more existing or newly formed companies'.

In both the above cases the transferor company is compulsorily dissolved without being wound up.

A partial asset transfer is a transaction whereby a company transfers, to one or more companies, the majority but not all, of its undertaking but where the transferring company is not dissolved or wound up.

In all cases the consideration for the transfer of the undertaking is the issue of shares in the transferee company to the shareholders of the transferor (except in the case of a partial asset transfer where the shares are issued to the transferor company itself). It is possible for up to one-tenth of the par value of the shares transferred (*soulte*) to be paid in cash.

The reorganisation may be notified to the Ministry of Economy or to the Competition Council but there is no mandatory requirement to do so as under the English Fair Trading Act 1973 (as amended by the Competition Act 1980).

One of the major and most difficult tasks in a re-organisation process is the valuation of the businesses involved in order to establish their relative economic 'weight' and thus to determine the amount of consideration due. The parties are free to choose any amongst the different available methods of valuation such as market value, liquidation value (market value minus taxes and duties due on a winding-up of the company), or intrinsic value. However the COB (*Commission des Opérations de Bourse*) issues guidelines as to the most appropriate methods.

Once the valuations have been fixed the unit value of each company may be determined by dividing the value of each company by the number of shares or *parts* comprising its share capital. The transferee or merged company can then issue the appropriate number of shares to compensate the transferor or merging company (or their shareholders) for the transfer of the undertaking.

Where the actual value of the shares of the merged company exceeds their par value, the difference between the net asset value of the assets received and the amount of the increase in its share capital is treated as a merger premium (*prime de fusion*).

It is usual for the shareholders of the merging company to have to exchange several shares or *parts* for one share or *part* in the merged company. Where shareholders do not hold the requisite number of shares or *parts* to entitle them to one share or *part*, since French law does not permit the issue of fraction shares, the shareholders must come to arrangements (*rompus*) amongst themselves to sell their shares or to buy more shares.

The proposed terms and conditions of a merger or hive-off must be contained in a written document (*projet de fusion ou de scission*) which must be signed by each of the parties.

The document must contain the following information:

    (i) the form, name and registered office of each company involved;

(ii) the reasons, the goals and conditions for the proposed reorganisation;
(iii) the dates of the company accounts used in setting up the operation;
(iv) the date on which the operations of the merging company will be deemed to be completed from an accounting point of view by the merged company;
(v) the procedure for transfer of shares including the date to which these shares should bear dividends;
(vi) the ratio of shares to be issued by the merged company to the merging company;
(vii) the amount of merger premium, if any;
(viii) and finally any rights granted to shareholders holding special rights as well as holders of any other securities other than shares and other special benefits enjoyed by the shareholders.

Where the undertaking transferred includes real property, the document must be signed before a notary (*notaire*).

The *projet* must be filed with the Commercial Court within the jurisdiction of which the registered office of each party is situated, at least one month before the first shareholders' meeting held to consider its terms. The document must also be published in the legal gazette for the department in which each party has its registered office.

In addition, in order to comply with the Third EEC Directive, the companies participating in a merger or a hive-off must file a Declaration of Conformity with the Commercial Court and Commercial and Companies Register in the jurisdiction of one of the merged companies. Here they must state that all necessary steps have been taken to comply with the relevant legal requirements.

Under the Law of 5 January 1988 the companies involved in a merger or hive-off (where the merging company is either a company limited by shares or a SARL) must apply to the court for the appointment of a merger or hive-off expert (*commissaire à la fusion* or *commissaire à la scission*) (most commonly the parties involved make a joint appointment) except where a company absorbs a 100 per cent subsidiary. The expert must prepare a written report analysing the proposed transaction for consultation by the shareholders. In the report the expert must check that the values attributed to the respective shares and *parts* are pertinent and that the share exchange is fair. The report must be made available to the shareholders at the registered office of the company one month before the shareholders' meeting called to approve the transaction.

The shareholders of each company must meet in extraordinary general meeting under the same conditions and according to the same rules and procedures applicable to an amendment of the companies' articles of incorporation. The board of directors or directorate of an SA must prepare a written report, explaining and justifying the re-organisation which must be made available to the shareholders before the meeting. They must also have the expert's report, the *projet de fusion*, the annual accounts approved in general meeting, the management reports for the preceding three accounting reference periods and a balance sheet dated no later than three months before the date of the *projet de fusion*.

The *fusion* or *scission* becomes effective from the date of the shareholders' meeting which finally approves the transaction where it involves existing companies or the date on which any new company (or the last company, if more than one) was registered on the Commercial Register. Where however the transfer takes place in a business which is subject to special state regulation such as insurance, any necessary consents should be obtained prior to transfer and a ministerial order (*arrêté*) will confirm the effective date of such transfer.

As a general rule, the merged company automatically acquires all the rights and obligations of the transferor arising from the re-organisation. Where the assets transferred include a commercial lease for instance, the merged company is substituted for the transferor and becomes the lessee by operation of law. Although employment contracts entered into by the merging company(ies) are also automatically transferred to the merged company this may not prevent redundancies which may be

Mergers

justified due to reduced staff requirements.

Any unsecured creditors of the companies involved in this type of re-organisation have the right to petition the competent *tribunal de commerce* for an order requiring the payment of all debts due at the time of publication of the *projet de fusion* or the *projet de scission* within 30 days of the publication. The court may either reject the claim or order its immediate satisfaction or failing that, order that the merged company give any necessary guarantees. The filing of claims by creditors in this manner does not prevent the parties from proceeding with the re-organisation. However, if the merging company does not comply with orders to reimburse or guarantee debts, the creditors will retain a preferential lien over the assets transferred to the merged company ahead of the new creditors of the merged company. Unsatisfied creditors of the merged company will retain preferential liens over the assets of this company ahead of the new creditors of the merged company.

There are special rules protecting secured creditors or holders of investment certificates (*certificats d'investissement*). These rules must be consulted on the subject of the re-organisation at a special meeting and they may be offered an option of becoming secured creditors or shareholders of the merged company or having their investments repaid. Failing this the creditors or shareholders may petition the court for an order for repayment of their investments or the granting of appropriate guarantees.

4.1.1 TAX TREATMENT

Re-organisations (including partial asset transfers concerning transfers of at least 75 per cent of the assets of the transferor) are given special tax treatment which is similar to UK tax law in the same circumstances.

Without this special system the tax consequences of the transaction would make it uneconomic. The transferor company would be deemed to have been wound-up and accordingly would be liable to pay tax on its untaxed profits prior to the re-organisation as well as on the capital gains it realised as a result of the transfer of its assets. It would also have to pay transfer duty (*droits de mutation*) on those liabilities transferred which are to be assumed by the merged company.

As a general rule, this special system applies to merged companies whatever their nationality. However, where transfers are made by French companies to foreign companies, the application of this special system requires the prior approval of the French Ministry of Economy. However, for registration tax purposes, approval is not required if the merged company has its registered office either in France or any other Member State of the EEC provided that the company is a *société de capitaux* by French standards.

The merger tax system only applies to transfers made by a foreign company to a French company which is subject to corporation tax (*impôt sur les sociétés*) if the foreign company is subject to a similar tax in its own country.

(1) Registration tax (*droits d'enregistrement*)

On a merger the transfer of assets is subject to a fixed charge of FF 1,220 and an *ad valorem* tax of 1.2 per cent of the difference between the net asset value of the transferor and the amount of its paid-up capital. This is payable by the merged company. A hive-off may be subject to the same tax treatment if it is first authorised by the Ministry of Economy.

Where the assets are transferred by way of partial asset transfer and constitute a complete branch of activity or are authorised by the Ministry of Economy they also benefit from this favourable tax treatment. However the 1.2 per cent *ad valorem* tax payable in connection with a merger is only due in special circumstances.

(2) Corporation tax (*impôt sur les sociétés*)

The merger tax system is only applicable in the case of hive-offs and partial asset transfers (unless the transfer constitutes a complete branch of activity and various conditions are fulfilled) where the prior consent of the Ministry of Economy has been obtained.

Under this system the transferor company is only taxed on the profits of the tax year immediately preceding the re-organisation plus any reserves which have not been used. In exchange for this concession the merged company must undertake to integrate into its taxable profits, in the five years following the merger, any capital gains arising as a result of the transfer of depreciable assets to the merged company. However in practice payment of the tax is generally spread over a period of time approximately equal to the depreciation period of the assets, so that no additional tax is effectively due.

The parties to the transaction are also given the option of paying tax on the long-term capital gains on depreciable assets at a reduced rate of 15 per cent on completion of the merger, without losing the benefit of depreciating the assets themselves.

(3) Income tax (*impôt sur le revenu*)

The issue of shares to shareholders or members of the transferor company on a merger is not deemed to be a taxable transaction for income tax purposes. The same applies to hive-offs and partial asset transfers where the prior consent of the Ministry of the Economy has been obtained in the conditions described above.

Any capital gain deemed to have arisen on the issue of the shares in the merged company to the shareholders of the transferor is subject to the usual rate for share transactions of 16 per cent.

4.2 ACQUISITIONS

4.2.1 ACQUISITION OF GOODWILL (*fonds de commerce*)

There is no legal definition of the term *fonds de commerce* however it is thought to combine the following elements:

Intangible elements:
–business mark;
–business name;
–occupancy rights under a lease;
–clientèle;
–intellectual property rights.

Tangible elements:
–stock;
–equipment;
–fixtures and fittings.

An asset acquisition is considered to be an acquisition of Goodwill if there is an explicit transfer of the constituent elements of the Goodwill the most important (and essential) of which is the *clientèle*. However, in certain circumstances a series of transactions may constitute an implied acquisition of Goodwill (even where the parties make no specific reference to this), for example:

(i) successive transfers to the same purchaser within a limited period of time, of the constituent elements of Goodwill;

(ii) the sale of a lease which necessarily results in the transfer of clientèle; or

(iii) the transfer of assets which necessarily enables the transferee to acquire a pre-existing clientèle.

The acquisition of Goodwill under French law is subject to a specific set of rules and has specific tax and legal consequences. The law provides that an agreement to purchase Goodwill must contain the following information intended to protect the purchaser:

(i) the name of the previous owner, the date and nature of the agreement pursuant to which the vendor acquired the Goodwill and the purchase price of the Goodwill;

(ii) a declaration of all liens, mortgages, security interests or other rights of third parties in the Goodwill;

(iii) the turnover of the business for each of the three years prior to the purchase;

(iv) a declaration of the net operating profit or loss, realised by the vendor during such period; and

(v) the date and duration of the lease, if any, relating to the Goodwill, as well as the name and the address of the lessor.

Acquisitions

It is worth noting that in the event of any of these pieces of information being omitted, the transfer of the Goodwill may, upon the application of the purchaser made within one year of the transfer, be declared null and void by the appropriate court.

The following formalities must be carried out with respect to the purchase agreement:
    (i) registration with the appropriate tax authorities and the registration duties (*droits d'enregistrement*) paid within one month of its execution;
    (ii) the publication of a notice containing details concerning the acquisition in the appropriate legal newspapers;
    (iii) the registration of the purchase agreement with the Registrar of Commerce and Companies;
    (iv) the filing of various declarations relating to social security, employment and VAT matters;
    (v) where appropriate, the registration of any vendor's lien with the Commercial Court.

The law provides that the vendor of Goodwill gives four implied warranties. It warrants that:
    (i) the representations contained in the purchase contract are true and accurate. If the vendor is in breach of this warranty, the purchaser may, within one year of the date on which he took possession of the Goodwill, bring proceedings against the vendor or any intermediary for either:
        —rescission and return of the purchase price; or
        —affirmation of the contract and damages for such misrepresentation.

        The purchaser will be entitled to punitive damages if he can prove that the representation was intentionally inaccurate.
    (ii) he will not set up in business in competition with the Goodwill. This warranty is implied by law but it is common to make specific arrangements in the purchase agreement which may increase its ambit. As, however, with all non-competition clauses it will only be enforceable if it is related to a limited territory and

is for a reasonable period.
- (iii) that the purchaser will have quiet enjoyment (*garantie d'éviction*); and
- (iv) that there are no defects in any constituent part of the Goodwill sold not discoverable by due diligence.

There are stringent requirements for publication of the agreement in order to inform any business creditors of the vendor and inform the tax authorities of the terms of the purchase. Publication must be in the appropriate legal gazette in the *département* in which the principal establishment is situated and any other *département* in which it has a branch, and in BODACC. Within the ten days following the last to appear of these two publications any creditor of the vendor may notify by *huissier* the purchaser and the clerk of the Commercial Court of any amount which he claims is due. Such notification (*opposition*) freezes the amount claimed in the hands of the purchaser until the merits of the claim are determined. As a result it is common practice for the purchase price to be paid into an escrow account held by a third party (usually a bank) who is identified in the advertisement and to whom any *opposition* can be notified.

Creditors have an additional right enjoyed by any interested party namely to bid for the Goodwill themselves. Such a bid must be for the advertised price plus one-sixth of the value of any intangible assets included in the Goodwill. The bid is notified by *huissier* in the same way as an *opposition* and is known as a *surenchère du sixième*. The purpose of this procedure is to protect creditors against artificially low sale prices. However in practice they are almost irrelevant.

The vendor may have a lien on the Goodwill (*privilège du vendeur*) if the purchase price is not paid in a lump sum on completion. Such a lien can only arise if the purchase agreement is in writing and has been registered with the Commercial Court within 15 days of its signature. The lien secures the vendor on the assets mentioned in the purchase agreement together with a maximum of two years' interest.

The sale of Goodwill will transfer by operation of law employment contracts and subsisting insurance policies and the right to occupy any premises attaching to it. The landlord of the premises must be notified by *huissier* of the sale unless he has specifically approved the transfer.

However, any permits or licences which are personal to the vendor will not be automatically transferred and the purchaser must ensure, prior to agreeing to purchase, that he will obtain the necessary authorisations himself.

Transfers of Goodwill are subject to a high rate of registration duty of 14.2 per cent of the price paid or the value determined by the tax authorities, if greater. The duty is normally payable by the purchaser and is a permitted business expense for tax purposes. However the vendor remains jointly and severally liable for any unpaid tax.

There has been a tendency to deal with the sale of Goodwill by crossed put and call options (*promesse unilatérale d'achat et promesse unilatérale de vente*). The option does not have to be advertised until it is exercised. The call option must be registered with the tax authorities within ten days of its exercise under pain of nullity of the option. Once exercised all the foregoing formalities relating to sale will apply.

4.2.2 LEASE OF GOODWILL (*Location-Gérance*)

French law permits the owner of Goodwill to lease out the bundle of assets and rights comprising it to a third party. (Law N° 56.277 of March 10 1956 amended by the Decree 86.465 of 14 March 1986). An owner letting out his Goodwill must be an individual *commerçant* or company which has carried on commercial activities for at least seven years and has run the business in question for at least two years. The prospective lessee must be a *commerçant* or a commercial company. The agreement will need to be published and will therefore need to be in writing. It must be registered with the tax authorities within one month of signature. The lessee-manager (*locataire-gérant*) runs the business at his sole risk and with full authority and pays a royalty fee (*redevance*) to the owner. This is subject to VAT. The owner will remain jointly and severally liable for the debts of the business for six months after publication of a legal advertisement giving details of the contract in a legal gazette or BODACC and it is therefore in his interests to advertise sooner rather than later. As with a partial asset transfer, the owner will remain jointly liable for any direct taxes arising from the running of the business for three months from registration.

Since no registration duty is payable in respect of a *location-gérance* contract, it is popular for prospective purchasers of Goodwill to enter into such an arrangement prior to a firm purchase since it gives them real experience of performance under their management. It is also popular with administrators appointed in winding-up proceedings (see Chapter 11). At the end of the period the Goodwill could be purchased or if not it will revert to the owner. There is no automatic right to renew but the same care needs to be exercised if a renewal is not envisaged as we will see in relation to commercial agency agreements, exclusive distributorships and franchises not to give any misleading indications as to renewal in order to avoid a claim arising for oppressive use of a contractual right (*abus de droit*).

French tax law contains anti-avoidance provisions designed to catch a concealed sale of Goodwill masquerading as a *location-gérance* (Tax Procedure Code art L64).

4.3 SHARE ACQUISITIONS—PRIVATE COMPANIES

There are no specific texts which govern the acquisition of interests in unlisted companies, even a controlling interest. That being so, a purchaser may rely on provisions of the general law contained in the Civil and Commercial Codes relating to the sale and purchase of assets. However, a share sale and purchase agreement is one of the contracts which should, in fact, receive the greatest care in its drafting and which can justifiably be based on Anglo-Saxon models. Many of the representations and warranties which commonly occur in an Anglo-Saxon agreement will be relevant although French draftsmen frequently have recourse to portemanteau terminology to which the courts will give effect, not least because of the implied obligation of good faith between the parties to the contract. Thus a guarantee of any diminution in the value of assets or increase in liabilities arising from matters undisclosed in the contract is known as a *garantie de passif* and can be drafted in far fewer words than in an Anglo-Saxon contract. A number of key points are set out below which are not exhaustive but will point up any significant differences from Anglo-Saxon practice. The same care needs to be exercised in France as anywhere else but special attention must be paid to the drafting of agreements since as a general rule representations made in pre-contractual negotiations other than in the clearest written terms may not be usefully referred to in any subsequent dispute.

(1) The same sort of information requires to be filed in France as in England with the Companies Register, the Land Registry and any other relevant trade bodies to which a target company is a member. In this way quite a detailed picture of a target company can be built up quite independently of any information which it may supply itself.

(2) French law is much more formalistic in relation to the capacities of signatories (see Chapter 3). However the PDG has actual authority to bind the company and does not require a board resolution to authorise him to contract on the company's behalf.

(3) The duty of good faith referred to above may mean that expenses incurred in abortive negotiations can be claimed if one party has acted in bad faith in breaking off negotiations.

(4) Control of French companies depends on having the appropriate majority and although 51 per cent is generally sufficient to control the day-to-day activities, enhanced majorities are required for certain extraordinary resolutions and the *statuts* of the company may contain specific restrictions. Read the latter with care and make sure that you understand the niceties involved, particularly in relation to the pre-emption rights of existing shareholders and the possibility that unanimity may be required for certain

decisions particularly in relation to a *société de personnes*.

(5) Bear in mind any relevant tax considerations and make sure that your proposal reflects them at any early stage. The introduction of a substantial re-working of the structure, solely for tax reasons, at a late stage will frequently be a problem. As we have seen there are tax and duties in France which do not exist in England such as those relating to a transfer of a *fonds de commerce*, which are substantial and although the transfer of control of a company by the acquisition of shares will not attract that duty, if the deal is complex, it may be relevant. On the other hand there is a lower rate capital gains tax for individuals on the sale of *actions* of 16 per cent and this may also be relevant.

(6) The price per share needs to be determined or determinable by reference to the contract for the contract to be enforceable. If there is an 'earn-out' component to the price, care must be exercised in this area. The price may be index-linked provided that the index chosen has a direct link with the activity of one or more of the parties or the subject matter of the agreement. Reference to the general Retail Prices Index will not normally be acceptable.

(7) Have regard to any exchange control clearance or ministerial filing or consent. Be aware also of mandatory consultation requirements for employees. A change of control requires consultation with the *Comité d'Entreprise*. Such a committee will generally exist in any business having more than 50 employees and a sale which has not undergone this formality is null and void.

(8) Obtain a *garantie de passif* from the vendors which is sufficiently detailed and long in point of time to cover any relevant prescription period especially in relation to tax liabilities. If the vendor is a corporation with

limited liability the shareholders may usefully be invited to co-guarantee. If future competition is relevant obtain a non-competition clause from the vendors and/or the shareholders but make sure that it is reasonable and enforceable.
(9) If any contracts of employment have to be terminated as a result of the sale, particularly those of board members make sure that terms have been agreed and the relevant resignations are in place on completion together with the appointment of any new directors.
(10) There is an unavoidable 4.8 per cent stamp duty on the transfer of *parts*. There is also a 1 per cent stamp duty on a contract to transfer shares in an SA. Unlike the tax on a transfer of *parts* the 1 per cent duty is territorial and the bona fide signature by the parties to the contract outside France will avoid it. Similarly the mere signature of a stock transfer form (*ordre de mouvement*) is not stampable.
(11) Bear in mind the application of any relevant EEC or National Competition Law or Mergers or Monopolies legislation (see Chapter 2 & section **4.4.4**).

4.4 ACQUISITION OF A PUBLIC COMPANY

As in England the acquisition of a minority interest in a public company does not require any specific authorisation by any third party. However, the acquisition of control, either in value or voting rights (*bloc de contrôle*), or any takeover bid is subject in France to specific regulations which are policed by the Stock Exchange Commission (*Commission des Opérations de Bourse*) known as the 'COB'.

4.4.1 COB

The COB was set up in 1967 and was modelled on the American Securities and Exchange Commission. However it does not have a mandate or powers as extensive as the SEC. These were, however, substantially extended by the Law of 2 August 1989 and deal with businesses in difficulty. It has ten members and its President is appointed by the Minister of Finance. Apart from its role, in relation to public company acquisitions, it has responsibility for listing and the proper functioning of the Stock Exchange (*bourse de valeurs*), sometimes known as the *Palais Brogniart*.

4.4.2 ACQUISITION OF A *BLOC DE CONTRÔLE*

This is a simpler procedure than a full bid and applies whenever control is acquired other than through the bid procedure dealt with below. Whenever control is to be acquired an application has to be made to the COB and an official announcement made in the Stock Exchange List offering to acquire from any shareholder his shares at the same price paid for the *bloc de contrôle*. This offer must be valid for at least 15 sessions of the Stock Exchange from the date of publication.

The application which is filed with the COB must set out the identity of the buyers and sellers of the *bloc de contrôle*, the date of the proposed transaction, the total quantity of stock to be purchased and the price to be paid. The COB must approve the terms and conditions and rule on whether it constitutes a *bloc de contrôle*.

Plainly the purchaser will not know in advance how much stock is going to be offered to him and is therefore somewhat of an open-ended commitment. There is no definition of what constitutes control but a 33.3 per cent stake is now thought to be sufficient if there are no other bigger shareholders.

4.4.3 TAKE-OVER BIDS

Anyone seeking to acquire a public company for cash (*offre publique d'achat* OPA) or shares (*offre publique d'échange*—OPE) is required to disclose and file certain information before the bid is mounted.

There are three organisations involved:
 (i) the Stock Exchange Council (*conseil des bourses de valeurs*) which analyses the price offered for the securities to be acquired;
 (ii) the COB which ensures that the bid information is full

and accurate and that the transaction complies with all applicable law and regulations; and

(iii) the Takeover Council (*conseil de surveillance des offres publiques en bourse*) which is composed of the Presidents of the Treasury Department, the COB and the Stock Exchange Council and which co-ordinates the activities of the two other organisations in relation to the bid.

There are detailed rules and regulations governing bids contained in the COB Rules of 28 September 1989. These regulate three types of bid:

(i) a full bid which will inevitably lead to a change of control;

(ii) a partial bid which aims for a public acquisition which will not transfer control;

(iii) the public acquisition of outstanding shares by an existing controlling shareholder.

The various rules are similar to the Yellow Book requirements of the London Stock Exchange but are beyond the scope of this work.

There are civil and criminal sanctions if the rules and regulations relating to public company transactions are not observed. The COB has powers similar to the Department of Trade in relation to the investigation of irregularities and may bring proceedings in its own name. If it is of the opinion that a criminal offence has been committed it will refer the matter to the equivalent of the Director of Public Prosecutions (*Procureur de la République*). In this context it is usually the COB which investigates and deals with allegations of insider trading (*délit d'initié*) which, as in England, is a criminal offence with similar consequences.

4.4.4 ANTI-TRUST PROVISIONS

Pursuant to the EEC directives in this area (Chapter 2), French law contains a specific Ordinance of 1 December 1986 which deals with the acquisition of interests likely to create a dominant position (*concentration*). This is similar to a reference to the Monopolies and Mergers Commission. This function is carried out by the Ministry of the Economy. These provisions relate to situations where more than 25 per cent of sales, purchases or other transactions relating to particular goods and services are controlled by a single company or group of companies as a result of an acquisition. There are also turnover thresholds.

Notification is not mandatory (as for Mergers—see *ante*) but plainly desirable since the Minister may modify or order the unwinding of a transaction which is considered anti-competitive. Any proposal or operation which is referred to the Minister will be approved if a ruling has not been made within two months of notification or six months if the Minister seeks the opinion of the Competition Council (*Conseil de la Concurrence*).

5
AGENCY

5.1 Background

The diversity of economic life is reflected in the many categories of intermediaries in commerce and industry, on the one hand commercial agents, *agents d'affaire*, commission agents and brokers who are considered in French law to be independent and on the other hand sales representatives who are employees and for this reason, subject to French employment legislation. The latter are considered to have a role which is subordinate to and dictated by their employer.

It is difficult to trace a dividing line between these various categories unless a distinction is made as to whether their members have a separate recognised legal status or not and whether they are independent or not.

5.2 Commercial agents

The commercial agent's profession is regulated by the Decrees of 23 December 1958 and 22 August 1968. The commercial agent's position is similar to that of an agent acting under a specific mandate and governed by art 1984 of the Civil Code. However the two Decrees mentioned above provide specific protection to the commercial agent in the event that his principal terminates his agency agreement without due cause.

According to the definition given by art 1 of the Decree of 23 December 1958, a commercial agent (*agent commercial*) is an individual or legal entity who carries on 'ordinarily' and 'independently' and 'professionally' (and otherwise than as an employee) the activity of the negotiation or conclusion of contracts for the sale, purchase or letting on lease or hire of goods or other property or the provision of services, for and on behalf of manufacturers, producers or merchants. According to the Decree, the commercial agent is defined as a representative (*mandataire*) and thus may be distinguished from a commission agent (*commissionnaire*) who acts in his own name on behalf of a principal (*committant*).

The agreement by which the principal appoints a commercial agent (known as a 'commercial agency agreement') must be in writing and must set out their respective capacities in clear terms.

Equally, in order to benefit from the specific protection which the Decrees afford, the commercial agent must be registered with the local Commercial Court (*tribunal de commerce*).

In this context it is useful to remind ourselves of the distinction in French law between civil and commercial contracts. The Decrees of 1958 and 1968 do not deal substantively with this issue. Nevertheless, it is important, particularly in determining the competent court in case of dispute between the agent and his principal. This controversy seems now to be settled, since the Supreme Court has clearly held that a commercial agency agreement is civil in nature. (Cass. Civ. Comm. 29 October 1979 and Cass. Civ. Comm. 28 October 1980.)

However, there is, in fact, simply a mismatch depending upon which party is plaintiff and which defendant in any dispute. Accordingly, the agreement is considered 'civil' for the agent and 'commercial' for the principal not least since the latter must be 'manufacturer, producer or merchant' in the definition given by the decrees and thus a *commerçant*.

If, therefore, an action is brought by the principal against the agent, the proceedings may only be brought in the Civil Court. If the action is brought by the agent against the principal, on the other hand, the competent court will be either the Civil Court or the Commercial Court at his option.

Because of this duality of jurisdiction it is not possible to have a valid arbitration clause in commercial agency agreements.

5.2.1 PERFORMANCE OF THE CONTRACT

(1) Duties of the agent
Like any agent, a commercial agent has two main duties:
—to carry out his appointed tasks; and
—to account for his actions to his principal.

The agent is liable for failure to fulfil his duties in the same way as an ordinary agent. However, the negotiation or conclusion of a contract by a commercial agent does not make him liable to third parties who deal with him if they know he is an agent and the acts in question are within the scope of his authority. In such a case, the third party has no recourse against him if the principal defaults on the contract.

The commercial agent's remuneration is called *commission* and is usually calculated as an agreed percentage of the gross or net total of the invoice value of orders obtained by the agent. This *commission* is intended to cover the expenses which the agent incurs in connection with his activities on the principal's behalf.

In principle, the commercial agent's right to commission crystallises when the relevant contract with a customer has been negotiated or concluded unless the commercial agency agreement specifies that the commission is due only when the relevant transaction has been fully completed or full payment is made to the principal. Clarity in the drafting of such provisions is obviously essential.

The commercial agent may represent other principals or may have an exclusive arrangement. In the former case, a commercial agent may not represent two competing principals and must receive his principal's prior authorisation. In the case of exclusivity, such provisions present the danger that the commercial agent be deemed to be so dependent on his principal that the commercial agency agreement is considered by the court or the Social Security authorities as an employment contract and thus subject to employment legislation. The consequences of such a re-characterisation are considerable since employers' Social Security contributions in France are high, with a top level of about 40 per cent of salary.

The commercial agency agreement may limit or prohibit the commercial agent's ability to appoint sub-agents or, on the contrary, may specify that the commercial agent must appoint a fixed number of sub-agents.

The commercial agency agreement may require the commercial agent to guarantee to his principal, the due performance of the agreement concluded on his behalf in return for a greater commission. Such an arrangement is known as *del credere* or a *convention du croire*. This is similar to the *del credere* agent familiar to English agency law. However, the French court has decided that a *del credere* agent not only guarantees payment of the price due by the buyer, but also guarantees the performance of other obligations such as delivery of goods. This agreement must be in writing since the contract is considered a civil one and the more liberal means of proof in commercial cases are not available. However, he is not liable for the negligence or other faults of his declared principal.

The commercial agency agreement may also contain a consignment clause (*convention de consignation*) pursuant to which the commercial agent is liable for the products placed at his disposal by his principal.

(2) Duties of the principal

The principal is liable if he does not fulfil his obligations as set out in the contract. Consequently, complaints, rejections of goods and claims notified to the commercial agent by customers must be forwarded by the agent to his principal.

As a general rule, as in England, the principal is liable to third parties for the acts of his commercial agents only if these are made within the scope of the commercial agent's authority. However, it has been held that a principal may be bound by commitments entered into on his behalf by commercial agents even though such commitments exceed the limitations set forth in the commercial agency agreement unless he can prove that the customer was aware of such limitations. It is sufficient that this be within the scope of his ostensible authority (*mandat apparent*). This will be a matter of fact in each case.

5.2.2 TERMINATION OF AGENCY CONTRACTS

(1) Termination for cause

A principal or commercial agent may terminate a commercial agency agreement for due cause without giving rise to a claim for damages or compensation. The expiration of the term or the non-renewal of a fixed term agreement, the death, the incapacity or the insolvency or bankruptcy of the commercial agent constitute due cause for termination. Equally, the commercial agent will not be entitled to termination compensation if the termination of the commercial agency agreement was justified by his improper conduct or breach of contract. The principal must prove that the agent has committed serious misconduct, justifying the termination of the agency agreement. However, the courts require a high standard of proof before permitting termination in such a case.

Whenever principal or agent seek to terminate a commercial agency agreement for cause, reasonable notice of such termination in writing must be given to the other party. If such notice is not acknowledged, due service must be proved and delivery by *huissier* is often a wise precaution.

(2) Termination without cause

The commercial agent is entitled to compensation for termination by the principal of his agreement without proper justification. In cases of unlawful termination, the agent has the right to receive 'compensation for the loss he has suffered' as a result of the termination (Decree of 1958, art 3). Any clause in an agency agreement excluding or restricting the agent's right to compensation in such a case is null and void.

Although there is no fixed rule for the determination of the amount of termination indemnity to be paid for the illegal termination of a commercial agency agreement, and although the court has a complete discretion to determine it, the indemnity is generally calculated by reference to the amount of commission paid to the agent during the previous two or three years.

5.3 INDEPENDENT AGENTS (*Agents d'affaire*)

Agents d'affaire are intermediaries who act in a similar manner to that of statutory commercial agents, but they are bound by a contract which does not fulfil the conditions imposed by the 23 December 1958 Decree for commercial agents.

Agents d'affaire are encountered in various fields of activity such as advertising, real estate, travel, insurance and the like and most of these professions are governed by specific statutes.

An agreement with an independent agent is considered by French law as a commercial mandate (*mandat commercial*) and unlike commercial agents, the activity carried on by independent agents is commercial and such agents have *commerçant* status.

The contract between an independent agent and his principal, which is purely consensual, need not be in writing or be evidenced in writing (Civil Code art. 1985), although if it is not, problems of proof may arise.

The independent agent is entitled to receive commission which is generally due only if the relevant transaction has been fully performed. The French courts consider that an independent agent has an obligation to make proper enquiries and to give advice to his principal. Such obligations may be enforced.

In addition to the usual events of termination of an agent's authority (such as agreement between the parties, the death of the principal or agent, bankruptcy or insolvency, etc), the agency comes to an end if the principal simply terminates the agent's authority. However, where the court is persuaded that the agency is one where there is a common interest (*mandat d'intérêt commun*), in the absence of an express agreement that the agent will have no right to compensation on termination other than for fault, the courts generally award compensation for termination. The existence of a community of interest between the principal and commercial agent may be proved, for example, by showing that both the principal and the agent have an interest in seeing an enterprise succeed by the creation and development of *clientèle* or, more specifically, by showing that the agent's remuneration is calculated by reference to a share of the profits of the transaction.

In such a case, the agent will be entitled to damages for the unjustified unilateral termination of his authority by his principal because of the parties' common interest in the performance of the agency agreement. Care needs to be exercised in drafting agency contracts to avoid these pitfalls.

5.4 COMMISSION AGENTS (*Commissionnaires*)

There are two kinds of commission agents: a purchase commission agent (*commissionnaire à l'achat*) and a sales commission agent (*commissionnaire à la vente*).

Article 632 of the Commercial Code provides that 'the undertaking of a business transaction on commission' is a commercial act, and so a person who habitually carries out transactions on commission is considered to be a *commerçant* and must therefore be registered.

Article 94 of the Commercial Code defines a commission agent as 'a person who acts for a principal but in his own name or in a business name'.

The commission agent's agreement with his principal is commercial and therefore, in the absence of a written contract, the agreement may be proved by any available means. Since the commission agent's agreement is deemed to be personal in nature, it will come to an end, like a *mandat* on the death, bankruptcy or insolvency of either principal or agent and also on the winding-up of a company which acts as principal or agent.

On the other hand, the commission agent's agreement cannot be terminated by the principal unless he indemnifies the agent for the liabilities and expenses he has incurred and for the value of the services he has rendered.

Unlike the commercial agent, the commission agent is a party to the contract he concludes on his principal's behalf and consequently he is personally liable to third parties with whom he contracts. Therefore, a selling agent may undertake the seller's obligations to the buyer, in particular, the implied undertaking that there are no hidden defects in the goods sold.

If the commission agent fails to follow his principal's instructions, the principal is not obliged to ratify the sale or purchase agreement executed by the commission agent and therefore leaves the latter personally bound.

In every commission agency agreement, the principal relies on the agent to use proper skill and care and to act in good faith in the principal's best interests. However, a commission agent does not guarantee to his principal that the person with whom the agent contracts on the principal's behalf will fulfil his obligations. However, a *del credere* provision may be inserted in any commission agreement in the same way as in a commercial agency agreement (see section **5.1.1 (a)**).

Since the principal is not a party to the contract made by a commission agent, third parties cannot take action against the principal in order to obtain execution of the contract. On the other hand, the principal has no direct action against third parties. However, art 1166 of the Civil Code provides for an indirect action (*action oblique*) subrogating the plaintiff to the claims of the agent against his principal or against the other party to the contract, as the case may be.

In addition to an indirect action, an action for unjust enrichment (*enrichissement sans cause*) may be brought by a purchaser against the principal where goods or services have been paid for, but no corresponding goods or services have been delivered or provided.

5.5 BROKERS (*Courtiers*)

Article 74 of the Commercial Code provides: 'the law recognises intermediate agents for carrying out commercial transactions, namely exchange dealers and brokers'. While some broking transactions are regulated in detail by law, for example those carried out by ship brokers and marine insurance brokers, others merely require the brokers who negotiate them to be registered with their regional Court of Appeal. This is the case with commodity brokers who engage in the public auction of goods in bulk and the enforcement of securities over goods and merchandise. On the other hand, most kinds of broking transactions are not subject to any legal regulation in the public interest, and practitioners in these areas are known as free brokers (*courtiers libres*). A broker is a person who makes his living by bringing together persons who wish to enter into a particular kind of contract, for example, sellers and buyers of a commodity.

Any person may carry out broking transactions, but art 1 of the Commercial Code provides that only persons who carry out such transactions habitually are *commerçants*. Brokers are independent and entitled to a commission.

A broker's obligation to his client is one of good faith and due diligence in the performance of his duties. The rate of commission to be paid is freely negotiated between the parties.

The client is obliged to pay the agreed commission to the broker as soon as a contract has been concluded with a third party found by the broker. In the absence of an express agreement to the contrary, the client must pay the commission, even if the person found by the broker fails to perform or becomes insolvent after the signature of the contract. It is only avoidance of the contract *ab initio* which will give rise to an obligation to return commission.

5.6 SALES REPRESENTATIVE (*Voyageur représentant placier*)

A sales representative (VRP) is a commercial representative employee (*salarié*) who visits his employer's clients within a specific geographical area in order to obtain orders which he transmits to his employer, for the latter's goods or services. It is important to note that since a sales representative is an employee and not an independent contractor, if he is employed in France by a foreign employer, the latter may be deemed for tax purposes to have a permanent establishment in France with all the usual consequences of such a finding.

If an individual satisfies the above definition, he benefits from the specific employee protection contained in the EC which guarantees him, *inter alia*, preferential working conditions and substantial compensation on termination of his employment.

All sales representatives must obtain a professional representative's identity card, which is delivered by the *Préfet de Police* of their home address.

Since the sales representative's function is to prospect for clients in the sales territory and to generate continuing relationships between such clients and his employer, the employer may benefit from the work done by the sales representative after the termination of the contract.

Consequently, under certain circumstances, the sales representative is entitled under French law to:

(i) earn commissions on orders placed after the termination of the sales representative's employment as a result of efforts he made in respect thereof (*commission sur échantillonage*);

(ii) subject to certain exceptions, an indemnity for existing *clientèle* (*indemnité de clientèle*); and

(iii) where the sales representative's employment agreement contains a non-competition clause, a special monthly payment (*contrepartie pécuniaire mensuelle spéciale*) for the period during which such non-competition clause is effective.

6
DISTRIBUTORSHIP

6.1 INTRODUCTION

A distributorship agreement is a purchase and sale agreement whereby the distributor is compensated for services by a gross margin on sales. Like franchise holders, distributors are given exclusive rights of distributorship for a specific product or range of products. In return distributors, like franchise holders, receive assistance from the manufacturer in organising sales and accompanying services, including technical 'know-how'.

No business activity can be carried on in an EEC country without taking into account the impact of community laws and directives. Distribution is no exception. The relevant provisions of the law in this area are dealt with in Chapter 2 together with relevant block exemptions.

There are three principal types of distributorship agreements in France. The first type of distributorship agreement is an exclusive distributorship agreement (*concession exclusive*) which grants, to the distributor, a monopoly within a specific geographical area on the sale of products furnished by the grantor.

The second type of distributorship agreement is created by a supply contract (*contrat d'approvisionnement*) pursuant to which the distributor agrees to purchase certain goods or services only from the grantor.

The third type of distributorship agreement is a non-exclusive one which may be a selective distributorship agreement (*concession sélective*) or approved distributorship (*concession agréée*).

6.2 EXCLUSIVE DISTRIBUTORSHIP AGREEMENTS

6.2.1 VALIDITY OF EXCLUSIVE DISTRIBUTORSHIP AGREEMENTS

Under French law and, in particular, the Ordinance of 1 December 1986 (the 1986 Ordinance), exclusivity clauses in exclusive distributorship agreements must comply with the following rules relating to refusal to deal, price fixing, restraint of trade and the duration of the exclusivity. However, if a provision is struck down for failure to comply, the whole agreement will not fall unless the particular provision was expressed to be of the essence of the contract.

(1) Refusals to deal (*Refus de vente*)

An exclusive distributorship agreement usually provides that the grantor undertakes not to sell his products to any of the exclusive distributor's competitors within the territory. For his part, the exclusive distributor is usually obliged not to sell products which compete with those of the grantor.

Such conduct inevitably results in the grantor eliminating a measure of competition within the territory by refusing to deal with other 'would-be' sellers of his products.

Such conduct is characterised as a 'refusal to sell' and it is considered illegal when a producer, trader, manufacturer or artisan unjustifiably refuses to accept an order placed by a professional for goods or services even though such order is in the normal course of business and placed in good faith. However, a refusal to sell is lawful if:

(i) it is permitted by a legislative text or regulation promulgated in application thereof; or

(ii) the seller can show that it is beneficial to the Economy (1986 Ordinance arts 10(1) and 36(1)(2)).

Certain types of agreements, such as those designed to improve the management of small and medium-sized businesses, may be authorised by a decree issued after consultation with the Competition Council (*Conseil de la Concurrence*).

Unfortunately, no regulations have yet been issued pursuant to the 1986 Ordinance and we have to assume for the time being that the cases under the prior

law are still valid. On that basis a refusal to deal is lawful if:
  (i) the exclusivity arrangements in the agreements are reciprocal.
  (ii) the territory where exclusivity is granted is precisely determined, and
  (iii) there are objective improvements in service to the customer which arise from the arrangement such as the distributor's ability to give technical assistance and service.

However, a grantor may not prohibit another distributor in another area or a third party purchaser of his products from selling in the exclusive territory.

(2) Price-fixing

It is unlawful to impose, directly or indirectly, a minimum price for the resale of goods or products or the rendering of services or to impose a minimum profit margin.

(3) Restraint of trade

Under French law, anti-competitive practices that result from a broadly-defined express or implied agreement and which affect the sale of goods or services in France are prohibited. Thus, an exclusivity clause has been considered an illicit restraint of trade, where it prohibits distributors from selling the grantor's goods in each others' territories and thereby eliminates all 'intra-brand' competition (Cass. Crim 1973 D.S. sur 677).

(4) Duration of the exclusivity

The duration of an exclusivity clause contained in an exclusive distributorship agreement relating to the sale, transfer or rental of goods may not, by law, exceed ten years.

6.2.2 OBLIGATIONS IMPOSED ON THE GRANTOR AND ON THE EXCLUSIVE DISTRIBUTOR

In addition to the general obligations imposed on the parties to an exclusive distributorship agreement which are pre-conditions to its validity, French law also imposes certain specific obligations.

(1) Obligations imposed on the grantor

The grantor is obliged to fulfil orders submitted in good faith by the exclusive distributor at the prices, and upon the conditions, set forth in the exclusive distributorship agreement.

The grantor must neither undermine the credit of the exclusive distributor nor act in such a manner as to lessen his Goodwill. The grantor is bound by an implied warranty (*garantie du vendeur*) against manufacturing defects in products sold by the exclusive distributor. The grantor is obliged to give a warranty of quiet enjoyment (*garantie d'éviction*) for the products sold to the exclusive distributor.

Most exclusive distributorship agreements oblige the exclusive distributor to permit the grantor to ensure that the obligations imposed upon him are fulfilled. If the control which the grantor exercises over his exclusive distributor is either insufficient or excessive the grantor may be held jointly and severally liable with him for his liabilities to third parties. This could arise (say) where the grantor has given the impression, by his conduct, that there is an identity of interest with the exclusive distributor (1965 JCPC1 No. 76218).

(2) Obligations imposed on the exclusive distributor

Pursuant to the exclusive distributorship agreement, the exclusive distributor may be obliged, *inter alia* to:

(i) maintain a minimum stock of the products,
(ii) hire qualified sales and maintenance personnel,
(iii) have appropriate premises and, where necessary, showrooms,
(iv) attain minimum sales targets,
(v) take part in or conduct advertising campaigns, and/or

(vi) meet certain minimum standards of financial solvency.
(3) Termination of exclusive distributorship agreements

A distributor has no basic claim to the manufacturer's *clientèle*. As a result, the termination of a pure distributorship agreement does not trigger severance payments and/or damages except for termination without proper notice.

However, considerable care needs to be exercised in the drafting of the termination provisions of distributorship agreements. Generally, non-renewal of a fixed term agreement will not give rise to a claim, but if supplies continue after the fixed term the court will imply an agreement of indefinite duration thereafter. Many French agreements provide for automatic renewal (*tacite reconduction*) at the end of the term unless one of the parties has given advance notice of his desire not to renew. If no specific period is stated, reasonable notice must be given. All notices should be given formally either by return receipt requested registered mail or *huissier*. It is advisable to give a generous notice period, even if none is specified, since too short a period will be ignored. The French notion of *abus de droit* is also relevant and representations that an agreement would be renewed if the distributor achieved certain targets, were held to give a claim in damages when the agreement was later not renewed although the target had been met (1978 Rev. Tri. Dr. Com. 593). If an agreement is for an unlimited period it should specify a notice period for termination. If it does not, termination will still be possible if reasonable notice is given.

The foregoing remarks apply where termination is required independently of breach of the agreement. French law will permit unilateral termination for breach (*résiliation unilaterale*) if the facts are sufficiently clear and the breach sufficiently serious. Alternatively the court may be asked to make an order terminating the contract (*résolution judiciaire*) if the matter is in real contention or doubt. Since a claim for wrongful repudiation may be substantial, especially if the agreement has subsisted for some time, legal advice should be sought at an early stage before deciding the course to adopt.

6.3 SUPPLY CONTRACTS

An exclusive supply contract (*contrat d'approvisionnement exclusif*) obliges the distributor to purchase products which he resells only from the grantor, but does not require the grantor to sell his products only to the distributor. It is for this reason that such contracts are sometimes referred to in France as contracts providing for unilateral exclusivity (*exclusivité unilatérale*). This type of contract is often used in connection with the distribution of gasoline and other petroleum products as well as beverages.

The rules governing supply contracts are similar to those applicable to an exclusive distributorship agreement, including the relevance of EEC law.

6.4 NON-EXCLUSIVE DISTRIBUTORSHIP AGREEMENTS

6.4.1 SELECTIVE DISTRIBUTORSHIP AGREEMENTS

A selective distributorship agreement is an arrangement whereby the grantor agrees to supply, within a given geographical area, goods or services to one or more distributors whom he selects according to objectively verifiable qualitative criteria without discrimination and without unjustified quantitative limitations.

Therefore a refusal by the grantor to sell his goods or services to third parties within the selective territory will be lawful only if the agreement involves products of high technology or a luxury nature, and the restriction does not affect the freedom that the distributors have in fixing the best price for their products. Thus the courts have upheld the right of perfumeries to supply their goods only to outlets of suitable standing (1983 Cass. Crim. D.S. Jur. som 211).

It follows that the grantor cannot object to sales of competing products or impose minimum prices (Cass. Civ. Comm. 1985 Bull. Civ. IV 143). Equally, if a potential distributor believes that he satisfies the objective criteria he may claim against a manufacturer who will not supply him on the basis of a refusal to deal (*refus de vente*).

6.4.2 APPROVED DISTRIBUTORSHIP AGREEMENTS

This type of agreement authorises a dealer (*distributeur agréé*) to sell products upon the footing that the manufacturer has specifically approved him. The grantor is free to supply other dealers and the dealer may sell competing goods. Care is needed by the manufacturer to avoid identifying too closely with any dealer since, as with exclusive arrangements, there is a risk of incurring joint and several liability for the dealer's acts or omissions.

7
FRANCHISING

7.1 BACKGROUND

A franchise agreement (*contrat de franchise/franchisage*) has many similarities to an exclusive distributorship and most of the comments made in Chapter 6 in relation thereto apply equally here including the relevance of EEC law and regulations. However, in as much as a franchise agreement applies not only to the supply of goods, but also services and the exploitation of know-how it is a closer relationship. French law has no separate body of legislation relating to franchising although it is mentioned in the Ordinance of 1 December 1986 (art 10(2)) concerning refusals to deal (*refus de vente*).

Accordingly, it is necessary to break down the agreement into its various aspects. The draft regulation of the EEC Commission on certain categories of franchise agreements 1987 LOCE No C 229/3 defines a franchising agreement as:

'an agreement whereby a business enterprise ("the franchisor") grants to another business enterprise ("the franchisee") in exchange for monetary consideration, the right to operate a franchise for the sale of goods to and the carrying out of services for end-users'.

The franchisee must display the franchise products in a way consistent with his co-franchisees, by using the same name or distinctive sign, the same know-how relating to the sale of goods or the carrying out of services to end-users. In this regard the franchisor gives to the franchisee uninterrupted commercial and technical assistance.

Accordingly the franchise agreement is not governed by a specific area of French law but rather the different areas of law governing the different types of contract which are grouped within it eg contract law, employment law, intellectual property law.

7.2 FRANCHISES AS LICENCES OF INTELLECTUAL OR INDUSTRIAL PROPERTY

The same rules apply to licences contained in a franchise agreement as generally (see Chapter 1). Specifically, if a trademark licence is involved it must be registered with the *Institut National de la Propriété Industrielle* to be enforceable against third parties. If the franchisee is a French tax-resident and the franchisor is not and the agreement contemplates transfers of industrial and intellectual property pertaining to technical or scientific assistance, this must be declared to the Industry Ministry within one month of signature of the agreement. Before 31 March in each subsequent year, a statement of royalties actually paid as well as accrued due and unpaid, must also be filed.

7.3 FRANCHISES AS KNOW-HOW TRANSFERS

As we have seen, know-how (*savoir-faire*) is protected in France (see section 1.4.2) and breach of confidentiality in this area will give rise to a damages claim, even if the know-how is transferred in contemplation of a franchise agreement which is subsequently not signed (Civil Code art 1382). The franchisor must supply the franchisee with the know-how he needs to perform his obligations pursuant to the agreement (Trib. Corr. Paris [1974] B.F.F.F. 209). The know-how concerned must be:
—original
—tested by the franchisor
—regularly updated
(TGI Bressuire (1974) DSJ 105)

7.4 CONTROL OF THE FRANCHISEE'S ACTIVITIES

As with exclusive distributorships, care must be exercised when checking on the franchisee's performance. Too little care may lead to allegations of negligence and too much may give rise to joint and several liability. Since the relationship between franchisor and franchisee is closer than that of manufacturer and distributor, the risk is greater.

7.5 EXCLUSIVITY

7.5.1 FRANCHISES

Franchises are *prima facie* a breach of art 85(1) of the Treaty of Rome. However, the draft block exemption referred to at section 7.1 above, envisages that they will be exempted if they benefit the consumer without excluding competition completely in a given area from other franchisees. In each case it is a matter of fact and degree.

7.5.2 PRONUPTIA LITIGATION

The decision of the European Court of 28 January 1986 in the Pronuptia litigation (CGCE 28/1/86: RTDE 86 p. 298) establishes the principle that in selecting a potential franchisee the franchisor may exercise special care, not least because of the confidential nature of know-how and trade secrets which form part of the agreement. His discretion is much greater than that of the manufacturer granting selective distribution rights, where the criteria have to be objective and generally applied (see section 6).

7.6 TERMINATION

The same care needs to be exercised in relation to the drafting of termination provisions in a franchise agreement and in their application, as in relation to other French contracts. Proper notice should be given in the appropriate manner and no representations should be made in the course of the contract inconsistent with the application of it, since as we have seen, the exercise of a legal right may be considered oppressive (*abus de droit*) in appropriate circumstances.

8
REAL PROPERTY AND SUCCESSION

8.1 INTRODUCTION

The purpose of this chapter is to deal briefly with the sort of land transactions which are most likely to be encountered. The main provisions of French succession law will be dealt with in the final section and in particular the forced heirship rules which will need to be borne in mind in commercial dealings with French individuals and corporations.

8.2 REAL PROPERTY

There are two types of transactions which it is necessary to know about, namely:
(1) sale and purchase; and
(2) leases.

The subject is vast and we shall have to limit ourselves to essentials and particularly essential differences. French law divides property and its attendant rights into personal (*biens meubles*) and real (*biens immeubles*). The distinction is important as it effects the way in which rights may be enforced and the jurisdiction of particular courts as well as procedural matters such as the need for publication or filing of contracts.

The classification contained in Civil Code art 517 depends not only on the nature of the property but also the purpose to which it is put or its relationship to other property; for example a life interest (*usufruit*) in a house is classed as real property as is an easement (*servitude*) over land. Fixtures and fittings are personal property unless they are so permanently fixed into place that damage would be caused either to the building or the particular fitting by its removal. The latter distinction explains why, when you take over real property at the completion of a purchase or a lease, there are scarcely any light bulbs and sometimes not even light fittings at all.

8.2.1 SALE AND PURCHASE

It is not necessary to know about rights of *usufruit* and indivision but he will need to be acquainted with both full freehold title (*pleine propriété*) and co-property interests (*co-propriété*). Although long leases (*baux emphytéotiques*) exist in France they are unusual; premises are often divided into units and sold to a plurality of purchasers to hold in perpetuity by virtue of a co-property arrangement, which is in some ways similar. The formal requirements for both freeholds and co-property are the same and therefore we shall deal with them both together and only distinguish them at the end of this section. All interests in land in France must be registered to be binding on third parties, although short leases are seldom registered since they generally only concern landlord and tenant.

The transfer of title to land is effected by an authentic document (*acte authentique*) executed before a notary. One notary may act for both sides or each may instruct his own. The transfer must deal with all aspects of the transaction and the purchaser's notary has a strict liability to obtain good title for his client. Similarly mortgages of land must be executed before a notary and contained in an *acte authentique*. There are anti-usury rules which limit the rate of recoverable interest and very strict rules of form and cooling-off periods which apply to residential property which are backed by criminal sanctions (these are contained in the *Lois Scrivener* see section **12.2(5)**).

A contract for the sale of land does not need to be by *acte authentique*. It usually takes the form of a unilateral contract for sale (*promesse unilatérale de vente*) whereby the purchaser agrees to buy for a price within a fixed period and the vendor agrees to sell. It is more like an option than a common law contract for sale. Unless he excludes his right to do so, the vendor may refuse to sell but will be liable to repay double the amount of the deposit paid. Failure to complete by the purchaser will result in the loss of his deposit. The period, usually about three months, between signature of the contract and completion is used by the notary to investigate title and purge the various rights of preemption that exist. Such rights are more circumscribed in the case of residential property in Paris but are commonly exercised by municipalities in and around Paris and in the provinces in the case if commercial property. These rights, which are given to the local commune of the sale of any land, enable the acquisition of banks of land to fulfil any local structure plan for the area or put together a development zone for housing or commercial use (see Chapter 13). The tax authorities have an analogous right which serves to discourage the unscrupulous from understating the true purchase price in the contract and transfer deed where a substantial cash payment is made in a separate related transaction. The state may acquire the property at 110 per cent of the contract price and the hapless purchaser, who will generally have paid his sweetener in advance, will get neither the property nor his money back. A true case of *caveat emptor*! This right of preemption may be exercised at any time within three months of registration of the sale.

The notary will also obtain a statement from the local council concerning the planning status of the property (*certificat d'urbanisme*)—this is valid for six months as to future matters and definitive as to the past. It will confirm, *inter alia*, that planning permission exists for any proposed development and states the existing use of the property. The vendor must produce an extract from the mortgage register (*état hypothécaire*) showing what, if any, registered mortgages there are or other encumbrances such as claims for arrears of tax, planning restrictions and such statutory matters. If some matter with a substantial impact on the property is revealed during this period the purchaser may withdraw from the transaction and recover any deposit paid. Thus the apparent swiftness and certainty of signing a purchase contract in France may be somewhat misleading on occasion.

The fees of the notary or notaries and expenses of the sale are usually all paid by the purchaser, although the parties are free to share them if they so agree. Registration duty is payable on completion in addition to the registration, search and notaries' fees. Registration duty (*droits d'enregistrement*) on commercial property is very high, currently 15.4 per cent of the purchase consideration. This has given rise to the practice of the ownership of property by means of a civil company (*société civile immobilière*) so that upon a sale of the shares of the company, the lower rate of duty applicable to such transfers of 4.8 per cent will apply. The cash saving obtained in this way is considerable and thought should be given at an early stage as to whether such a structure is appropriate for the purchaser as the property may be more attractive and potentially more valuable on resale. In view of the high cost of dealings in land of approximately ten per cent for residential property and 20 per cent for commercial, once arrangements have been put in place it is expensive to unwind them. Certain newly built property is subject to value added tax on its first sale at the appropriate rate as are certain derivative transactions relating to real property (art 257, TC).

Completion of a French sale and purchase is a proceeding which most people familiar with common law jurisdictions will find surprising. Since, as we have seen elsewhere, the French courts have considerable reservations as to the fair and honest dealings between individuals and companies, there is much formality which is designed to avoid the transaction being subsequently called into question. The notary dealing with the completion will be careful to verify the identity of the parties and ensure that they fully understand the transaction which usually involves laboriously reading through the transfer document which will generally be quite long. Payments will pass through the notary's client account (which is guaranteed by the profession) including, in most cases but not as a legal requirement, the deposit that was paid upon exchange of contracts. Care should be taken to ensure that all financial transactions are dealt with through the notary's account. This should include transfers of money from outside France as it will be proof of the foreign origin of the funds if this is later a material fact. The virtual abolition of Exchange Control has made such considerations less critical.

Real property in France may be subject to easements and other incorporeal rights which require registration to be binding on third parties, they are either statutory, legal or consensual. The former flow from a ministerial act and are therefore unilateral, the second arise by operation of law much as an easement of necessity arises in England and Wales and the latter by agreement. These should all be revealed in the purchase deed.

The vendor of real property in France gives only two warranties by law—namely quiet enjoyment (*garantie d'éviction*) and freedom from inherent defects (*garantie des vices cachés*) not discoverable by due diligence. The warranty of quiet enjoyment is absolute so far as the acts of the vendor and those claiming through him are concerned, but may be excluded as far as third parties are concerned if the parties so agree and this is commonly done. The vendor is free to seek to exclude the warranty of freedom from inherent defects, but this exclusion will not be effective if he is professionally involved in property ie builder or property dealer and if it can be shown that he knew or should have known of the defect at the time of the sale. If an operative hidden defect is discovered the purchaser may rescind the contract and claim return of the purchase price or affirm the contract and claim damages for the cost of repair or diminution in value. If rescission is chosen, damages may only be claimed additionally if the vendor knew or should have known of the defect at the time of the sale. There is a right which the vendor may exercise within two years of completion and after registration of the sale if he can show that the price paid was unconscionably low (*rescision pour lésion*). He must show that the price he received was less than five-twelfths of the fair market price at the time of sale. Curiously he is entitled to rescind even if such right was excluded by the contract. However, if the right to rescind on this ground is recognised the purchaser may pay the difference with interest, but calculated as a fraction at the date of payment, less a statutory discount of ten per cent of the total price.

Before leaving the subject of sale and purchase it is worth saying a few words about mortgages of land. France has strict formal requirements in this respect and failure to observe them renders the mortgage void. As far as consumer transactions are concerned, there are also criminal sanctions for lenders who do not comply. A statutory right accrues to a third party who lends money to finance a property purchase (*privilège du prêteur de*

denier) in certain circumstances which need not detain us. In a business context formal mortgages are more common. In order to be valid, the latter must:
   (i)   be contained in notarial deed,
   (ii) be signed in France,
   (iii) describe the exact nature and location of the mortgaged property.

To be conclusive as to the amount of the debt secured the mortgage must be in respect of a liquidated amount which is due. If the amount of the debt is not certain at the time of registration, the mortgagor may subsequently challenge the nominal amount.

Mortgages in France are registered in the mortgage registry by a special official (*conservateur des hypothèques*) and attract proportionate fees for the filing (*salaire du conservateur des hypothèques*) and its subsequent publication (*taxe de la publicité foncière*). They are only binding on third parties if properly filed and published. Mortgages of unlimited duration are not permitted. Generally the date specified in the mortgage for repayment will be the relevant date, although it is common to extend it for a further two years which is the maximum period allowed. The initial registration cannot however exceed thirty-five years in total. The registration may be renewed for successive periods upon payment of a further fee. The rights and remedies of a mortgagee are similar to those in England and Wales as are the ways in which a mortgage is discharged.

At the beginning of this section the distinction between freehold and co-property interests in land was mentioned and here is a convenient place to distinguish them, since in the next following section on business leases the tenure of the landlord is broadly irrelevant. Freehold title (*pleine propriété*) is equivalent, in all material respects, to its English equivalent connoting ownership in perpetuity of the land and subsoil. This includes any incorporeal rights, such as easements and subject to any easements or reserved rights that affect it, although there is no legal fiction of holding the land from the Crown. Co-property rights, however, are similar to the North American condominium but have no English equivalent as such. The relationship between the co-owners is similar to that between long leaseholders with the significant difference that there is no third party landlord to own the common parts and procure compliance with lease covenants. The common parts and indeed the site itself is owned by the co-owners (*co-propriétaires*) in undivided shares (*millièmes*) in a ratio determined by the co-property deed (*règlement de co-propriété*) which must be signed before a notary. Ownership of a co-property interest (*lot*) confers the right to the exclusive use and occupation of the *lot*. This is defined by the co-property deed but is subject to the terms of the deed which will regulate the relationship of all the co-owners *inter se*. The deed is a public document and is filed with the Land Registry. It may only be changed with the consent of a majority of co-owners and there are special rules that limit the right to modify certain aspects, or require enhanced majorities or even unanimity to modify specific matters or grant additional rights, such as the right to add further floors to an apartment building (*droit de sur-élévation*). Co-properties are generally managed by a professional property manager (*syndic de co-propriété*) although one of the co-owners may fulfil this function. There are requirements for a steering committee of co-owners and elaborate legal requirements concerning the calling of and agendas for meetings, all of which requirements are mandatory and may invalidate decisions which are taken. Any modification of the co-property deed requires to be signed before a notary and filed with the Land Registry. Co-property meetings should be conducted along the lines of shareholders' meetings of companies, although the latin temperament and the passion, which the ownership of interests in land engenders, can and frequently does make the proceedings very lively and animated. It is worth noting that if a co-property interest is purchased in a building with a large number of co-owners it may be, and often is, quite difficult to obtain the quorum necessary to vote on amendments to the co-property deed. Great care should be exercised when considering its terms before purchase as change may simply not be feasible.

8.2.2 BUSINESS LEASES

The law as it affects business leases is as complex and as important in France as it is in England and Wales. The business tenant, who is either French or an EEC national, generally has security of tenure and is entitled to compensation if his lease is not renewed in cases where the law so allows. This is, however, another area where the resultant provisions under both French and English law may be the same in effect but the legal thinking behind them is very different. Security of tenure for business tenants is linked to the notion of Goodwill (*fonds de commerce*) which is described in Chapters 3 and 4, and the status of the lessee as a commercial entity (*commerçant*). The law seeks to keep the tenant in his premises to preserve his *clientèle* and his Goodwill. As mentioned in the Introduction foreign business corporations are by definition commercial entities and thus entitled to protection. An individual however must be registered with the Commercial Registry and hold a trader's card (*carte de commerçant*) if he is not an EEC national. To be subject to the laws governing business tenancies the following three conditions must be satisfied:

    (i)   the lease must be of premises both used to exploit Goodwill and for commercial purposes (which includes workshops used by artisans and school premises).

    (ii) the term must exceed two years.

    (iii) the lessee must be a commercial entity.

If these conditions are satisfied then the provisions of Decree No. 53.900 of 30 September 1953 relating to the renewing of leases ('the 1953 Law') apply automatically and it is not generally possible to contract out of them. Where the term 'business lease' is used below it refers to one subject the 1953 Law.

As a general rule a business lease may not be for less than nine years. The lessee but not the lessor may terminate the lease at the end of each three-year period by giving six months' prior written notice to expire at the end of such a period. These are the most common business leases and are known as 3/6/9 for obvious reasons. It is however possible to contract out of triennial termination in favour of a fixed term. An individual business tenant who is retiring or who qualifies for disability allowance may terminate a business lease on six months' notice at any time.

There are anti-avoidance provisions relating to the renewal of a lease of less than two years which would otherwise be a business lease and any renewal thereof will bring it within the 1953 Law and must therefore be for at least nine years. If it purports to be for less, the court will construe it as 3/6/9.

Modern business leases are usually very specific as to the agreed use of the premises. The old all-purpose lease (*bail tous commerces*) is a thing of the past. The tenant must respect the user covenant strictly. There are special mandatory rules which apply to changes of such use.

The first concerns 'related or complementary activities'. A tenant wishing to add such activities must serve written notice by bailiff (*huissier*) upon his landlord. During the following two month period the landlord can challenge the nature of the activities in the courts. If he does not do so the tenant is deemed authorised and the landlord may, if it can be justified, be entitled to an enhanced rent at the next triennial review.

The second relates to the addition of a use or substitution of changed use. *Prima facie* there is no right to change the agreed user of premises, but there is a procedure whereby the tenant may serve written notice by bailiff upon his landlord requesting a change of use. If he has any registered encumbrances on his Goodwill, the mortgagee must also be served and can take steps to preserve his rights. If the landlord has other business tenants who might be affected by the change, they too must be similarly served with notice and have a month to object. The landlord must either accept or reject the proposal within three months of service. If he has done nothing, he is deemed to acquiesce. Furthermore he cannot unreasonably object to such a proposal. If he accepts or is deemed to do so he may claim compensation for any loss he has suffered as well as an increase in rent if it can be justified. The grounds for refusal are those which might be expected, incompatibility with the building or other uses to which it is put or prejudicial change which would occur in the neighbourhood.

He may, however, refuse, if at the end of the next following three-year period, he intends to seek possession for refurbishment or redevelopment, but in such a case compensation must be paid (see below).

The tenant under a business lease has no right to sublet the whole or part of the premises without the landlord's consent. To do so without consent can justify termination of the lease, either immediately or at the end of the lease, without compensation. If subletting is permitted, and it generally is not, there are certain formalities which must nonetheless be observed. This includes inviting the landlord by return receipt requested registered letter or notice served by bailiff to enter into the subtenancy for conformity and to have privity with the subtenant. The landlord will thus generally know if the subletting is at a profit rental and he is entitled to seek an increase of the head rent to reflect this. The head tenant remains jointly and severally liable for the rent. Upon expiry of the headlease it is the subtenant who is protected.

The tenant who exploits Goodwill in leased premises may, by law, freely transfer the right to occupy those premises to the purchaser of his Goodwill without the landlord's consent. The lease may, and most do, exclude any other assignment except in the case of a tenant who is retiring or one who now qualifies for certain disability allowances. In either of these two latter cases it is normal to provide that the landlord has a pre-emptive right to buy out the tenant's lease and, in any event, certain formalities must be observed by the tenant. An unlawful assignment will generally give the landlord the right to forfeit the lease.

There are currently no controls over business rents, although there have been in the recent past, and the parties are therefore free to negotiate the opening rent. Thereafter it is determined either by reference to indexation clauses which are common or, in case of dispute at a review or on renewal, by the court. There are statutory provisions which limit the court's right to increase the rent other than by reference to the published quarterly Construction Cost Index 'QCCI' (*indice trimestriel du coût de la construction*). A permissible triennial review cannot generally exceed three times the annual increase in the QCCI since the quarter in which the rent was last reviewed.

Where the operation of an automatic indexation clause, which for property must be by reference to the QCCI, has caused an increase or decrease of at least 25 per cent in the original rent payable, either party may petition the court for a revision of the rent to set it at the current fair market value of leased premises. Such a determination will relate back to the date of the request for it and once fixed the rent will be subject to indexation as before.

Where the parties cannot agree a new rent on renewal of a lease of nine years or less, the court will do so, at the request of either, by reference to comparables. Generally the increase is limited to the annual increase in the QCCI over the original lease term as a multiplier of the original rent. The local Conciliation Commission, which is composed of representatives of both landlords and tenants must also adjudicate on the request but if it fails to do so within three months its jurisdiction comes to an end. The court cannot decide the matter unless the Commission has adjudicated or failed to do so within the time allowed, but in any event neither party is bound by the Commission's finding. However, this cap on permissible increases does not apply, *inter alia*, to office premises. In the case of pure office user the parties must adduce expert evidence of comparables and in suitable cases the court will appoint a court expert to report.

A tenant who is the owner of the goodwill attached to business premises and who has been in occupation for at least three years prior to the expiry of the lease has the right to renew. If renewal is refused, he has the right to compensation unless the tenant is not a French or EEC national or national of a country giving analogous rights to French nationals.

There are complex procedural steps to be undertaken by either side to institute the renewal process and the new lease will generally be for nine years unless the parties agree a longer period. The landlord may refuse renewal on the grounds of serious breaches of the lease including non-payment of rent, late payment, unauthorised alterations or subletting and the like. In such a case no compensation is payable; as is the case when the landlord requires the premises himself either because they must be demolished as unsafe or unsanitary or he wishes to demolish and reconstruct a building on the site. The landlord must, however, offer the outgoing tenant reasonable equivalent accommodation.

If the landlord refuses to renew he must give notice by *huissier* specifying his reasons and notifying the tenant of his rights. If there is no valid reason, the tenant must nevertheless give vacant possession, but is entitled to compensation equivalent to the loss he will suffer from the non-renewal. In an appropriate case the damages claimed may be equivalent to the whole value of his Goodwill, which may be substantial.

If a landlord has obtained vacant possession upon one of the statutory grounds but in bad faith, he may face an action for damages by the evicted tenant.

8.3 SUCCESSION

There are a number of very significant differences between succession law in France and England both formally, since there is no need for executors and there are no will trusts, and in substance since the testator is not free to dispose of his estate as he wishes. Much of the arcane science associated with this subject is irrelevant in a business context, but it is worth noting that, if the deceased has children, only a portion of his estate may be left otherwise than to them. If he has one child half his estate must go to that child, if he has two, two-thirds must go equally to them and in the case of three or more three-quarters of the estate passes to them in equal shares. For all practical purposes it is impossible to disinherit a child. A surviving spouse has no automatic right to a share of the deceased spouse's estate, except in the case of intestacy without children or living parents. A surviving spouse may be given a life-interest (*usufruit*) in the whole of the deceased's estate and may be left the whole of the free estate (*quotité disponible*). The children will be left with the remainder (*nue propriété*) during their surviving parent's life. The children will normally hold undivided shares (*en division*) although a severing of the indivision (*partage*) is always possible.

Since much French business is done by corporations which are controlled either by a founding patriarch or a single family, the influence of succession law remains strong even if only as a background to the behaviour of the French parties involved. Indeed, upon the death of anyone in France gifts and disposals of assets other than for full value made by the deceased at any time up to thirty years (and arguably without limit in point of time) before the date of death, may be called into question if their value exceeds the free portion of the estate. The scope for complex litigation can be seen to be considerable. This factor coupled with a right to freeze assets by way of conservatory arrest (*saisie conservatoire*) which the courts are relatively relaxed about granting, may complicate ordinary business dealings to a substantial extent.

Although it is not strictly a matter of succession law, it is worth mentioning here the influence of the continental notion of marriage contracts (*régimes matrimoniaux*) as they affect business dealings. It is not necessary under French law to have a marriage contract (*contrat de mariage*) but if a couple does not have one they are deemed to be married under the regime of community of goods (*communauté des biens*) which means broadly that they each have a half share in the assets of the family. If another regime is chosen, typically the separation of goods (*séparation des biens*), each spouse keeps the assets brought to the marriage and any assets acquired thereafter. The French courts consider family law in England to mean that English couples have discrete assets in a similar way to separation of goods.

The distinction is important in business since a husband (or wife for that matter) married in *communanté* does not have full freedom, in certain circumstances, to deal with goods by way of sale without the other spouse entering into the contract or consenting in writing. The subscription of shares in companies is similarly affected as is the giving of any guarantee or surety. In the case of a civil company (*société civile*), which has unlimited liability, the subscription of shares upon incorporation by a spouse so married will invalidate the incorporation of the company without the other spouse's written consent (usually in the *statuts*).

It is hoped that the foregoing brief indication of some of the aspects of French family law will help to clarify idiosyncracy, which, without this background knowledge may seem quite bizarre. The latest peripatetic developments in the affairs of Gallimard S.A. make interesting reading for those wishing to see these problems in action.

9
IMMIGRATION AND EMPLOYMENT

9.1 IMMIGRATION

9.1.1 NON-EEC NATIONALS

(1) Right to reside

All non-EEC nationals who intend to reside in France for more than three months must apply for a temporary residents permit (*carte de séjour temporaire*) within eight days of their entry into France. This is issued by the *Préfecture* for the area in which the individual intends to reside, for a period of one year, and is renewable thereafter.

A full residence permit (*carte de résidence*) is granted to anyone who can prove, *inter alia*, that they have lived lawfully in France for a continuous period of three years. A residence permit is valid for ten years and is automatically renewable at the end of this period. It entitles its holder to both live and work in France.

(2) Right to work

   (i) Employee

An employer wishing to employ a non-EEC national to work in France on a regular basis as a salaried employee (*salarié*), must obtain authorisation for him to do so from the *Services de la main d'oeuvre*, before the employee arrives in France and make the relevant social security declarations. When making his application, the employer must file with the local Employment Agency (*agence locale pour l'emploi*), having jurisdiction over the employer's place of work, a copy of the employment contract together with other information about the person he wishes to employ. The agency then examines the application. If it decides to grant the application it issues an authorisation (*visa*) specifying the authorised activities and geographical area in which these are to be carried on and forwards this to the *Office des migrations nationales*. The latter satisfies itself as to the professional and medical suitability of the foreign employee by requiring him to undergo a medical examination before he leaves his country of origin.

Subsequently the employee must present his authorisation when applying for his *carte de séjour temporaire*, which will then be stamped with the word *salarié* and will enable the employee to carry on the activities in the geographical area specified on the authorisation.

For certain categories of temporary employee who are not entitled to receive a *carte de séjour temporaire* with the stamp *salarié* eg foreign students taking a sandwich course at a French university, a temporary work authorisation may be granted for a period of six months. This may be renewed subsequently.

(ii) Self-employed

In order to work in a self-employed capacity in the following capacities:

—sole trader (*commerçant*);

—*gérant* of an SARL;

—*associé* with unlimited liability for the debts of a *société* (eg in a SNC, SCS or SCA);

—PDG, DG, *Président du directoire* of an SA or director of a GIE who has the ability to bind the GIE vis-à-vis third parties

a non-EEC resident must obtain a foreign businessman's card (*carte de commerçant étranger*) from the *Préfecture* of the department in which

the *société* or GIE in question carries on its business.
- (iii) Professional

    A self-employed professional (*profession libérale*) wishing to carry on business in France follows the procedures set out in (ii) above except that instead of an employment contract he needs to procure some sort of approved consultancy agreement; otherwise he does not need a specific authorisation to work in France if his residence permit authorises him to reside and work in France.

9.1.2 EEC NATIONALS

Nationals of Member States of the EEC have the right to receive an EEC national residence permit (*carte de séjour de ressortissant d'un Etat membre de la Communauté Economique Européenne*) by filing an application at their local *Préfecture* within three months of their entry into France. They must also produce their foreign identity card or passport and various other documents. An EEC national residence permit is valid for five years and may be renewed as of right for successive periods of ten years.

EEC nationals do not need to seek authorisation to work in France as *salariés*, *commerçants* or *professions libérales*. Under the Treaty of Rome they are treated as French nationals for this purpose. They are, however, subject to the same restrictions on access to certain professions. In particular the giving of legal advice in France will be restricted to those qualified in France after 1 January 1992.

9.2 EMPLOYMENT LAW ISSUES

9.2.1 LEGISLATION

Relations between employees and employers are governed by the French Employment Code (*EC*), collective bargaining agreements (*conventions collectives*), internal company regulations (*règlements intérieurs*) and case law.

Collective bargaining agreements relating to a particular profession or trade are negotiated between trade union representatives and business federations or companies. They establish binding regulations relating to the terms and conditions of employment of staff ranging from recruitment and dismissal to employees' travel arrangements. French *conventions collectives* also contain specific provisions relating to the definition of categories of employee.

9.2.2　EMPLOYMENT CONTRACT

An employment contract may be of fixed or indefinite length. Indefinite term contracts are governed by the law of contract and may be oral or implied. However bearing in mind the inadmissibility in French court proceedings of oral evidence it is recommended that all employment contracts be in writing.

A fixed-term contract must be in writing and must specify the length of the term. It is worth noting that fixed-term employment contracts have only recently become legal and only then in specific circumstances such as the following:

- (i) where a permanent employee is temporarily absent and he must be replaced;
- (ii) where there is a temporary increase in business;
- (iii) where there is a need to fulfil a specific task;
- (iv) where there is a need to fulfil an exceptional order;
- (v) where a particular job is of a seasonal nature; or
- (vi) in the case of government work programmes designed to reduce unemployment.

With some exceptions, the term of a fixed-term contract may not exceed twenty-four months including any renewal. In the event of the employer/employee relationship continuing after the expiration of the fixed term, the employment contract automatically becomes an indefinite term contract.

As a general rule, upon the expiry of a fixed-term contract the employer may not enter into another fixed-term contract with another employee to fill the same position until a certain period of time has elapsed.

Until recently the ability of employers to employ temporary

staff was strictly limited and the activity of a temporary employment agency strictly regulated. Currently, an employer may only hire an employee on a temporary basis for the performance of a non-permanent task.

Employers may only employ temporary staff through temporary employment agencies by written contract. As a general rule, the term of a temporary contract may not exceed twenty-four months, including any renewal. The temporary employment contract is subject to the same conditions as those governing the fixed-term contract.

Employment contracts may contain a trial period during which either party may unilaterally terminate the contract. The party terminating the contract may not be held liable to the other party as a result of such termination unless such termination constitutes an *abus de droit*. (This is a concept which does not exist under English law and roughly translated means the exercise of a legal right in an oppressive way.) The trial period may be freely fixed by the parties to the contract, taking into account the relevant provisions of any collective bargaining agreements and trade practice. However the courts have the power to overturn such provisions if they consider them to be excessive.

Similarly an employee's salary may be freely fixed by employer and employee subject to the provisions of any applicable collective bargaining agreement. The minimum wage in France is known as the '*salaire minimum interprofessionnelle de croissance*' (or SMIC) periodically fixed by the government. As of December 1990, the minimum monthly wage was FF 5,398 for 169 hours. In addition to the employee's basic salary and overtime, the employer is obliged to pay certain bonuses and fringe benefits eg he must reimburse 50 per cent of the employee's travel expenses; it is also common in collective bargaining agreements to provide for incremental salary increases based on length of service (*prime d'ancienneté*).

In addition to obligations, vis-à-vis his employees, the employer has an obligation to indemnify third parties for injuries suffered by them as a result of the acts or omissions of his employees in the course of their employment.

Employers employing twenty or more people on a regular basis are obliged to prepare internal regulations (*règlements intérieurs*) which set four certain rules which their employees must respect in the performance of their duties. Such rules relate to health and safety matters or disciplinary rules and sanctions. Failure by the employee to respect these rules may lead to him being sanctioned. The most serious sanctions which may be imposed are the following:

(i) the suspension of the employee (*mise à pied*) for a period of time which must be fixed in the notice of sanction;

(ii) the demotion of the employee (*déclassement professionnel*) following which both the employee's duties and remuneration are changed;

(iii) the transfer of the employee (*mutation*) to another job or work site; and

(iv) the dismissal of the employee provided that this would not violate any applicable procedures.

In any of the above circumstances the employee may appeal to the appropriate employment tribunal (*Conseil des prud'hommes*).

Statutory provisions regulate the variation, suspension, and termination of employment contracts. The employee must accept variations of a minor nature made to his terms of employment by the employer. He may refuse, however, any major modification such as a decrease in his salary or responsibilities. Such a refusal may constitute a constructive dismissal by the employer and entitle the employee to bring an action for unfair dismissal. The employer will have a defence to such a claim if he can prove that the variation was an important consideration in maintaining the well-being of his business. In the event of the employer's legal status being varied following a sale, merger, transformation, or reorganisation, the employment contract will continue in force between the employee and the employer, or his successor. The latter assumes the obligations of his predecessor under the employment contract except in the case where the former employer was insolvent.

The termination of an employment contract governed by

French law is a complex affair. The general rule is that an employee may terminate an employment contract at any time either expressly or impliedly. The employer must continue to pay the employee his salary together with all other forms of remuneration due to him until the termination becomes effective including compensation for any accrued holiday entitlement which the employee has not taken.

However a fixed-term contract may not be terminated before the end of its term except in the event of gross misconduct (*faute grave*) or *force majeure*. Where a fixed-term employment contract pursuant to its terms is not extended, the employer is obliged to pay compensation (*indemnité de fin de contrat*) to the employee equal to no less than five per cent of the total gross salary received by the employee during the term of employment. However no compensation is payable where the employee resigns or is dismissed for gross misconduct or following an event of *force majeure*. If the employer wrongfully terminates a fixed-term employment contract, the employee is entitled to receive, in addition to the foregoing compensation, damages for wrongful dismissal. This must be equal to the salary he would have earned had the employment contract run its term plus damages for injury suffered as a result of wrongful dismissal (if any).

Conversely, the employer may terminate an indefinite term employment contract at any time. However if he does so without respecting the various rules and regulations designed to protect the employee, he may be liable to pay the employee a substantial amount of damages. In order to avoid payment of damages, the employer must be able to show that he had justifiable grounds for the termination (*cause réelle et sérieuse*) of the contract and has complied with all applicable dismissal procedures. The grounds for termination are not specifically defined by law but case law helps to define the circumstances which will justify dismissal. These include failure to perform on the part of the employee, loss of confidence in the employee etc.

Although the *Conseil des prud'hommes* may review and reverse other disciplinary sanctions imposed on the employee it may not order the employer to reinstate the employee against his will. Thus where it finds, for instance, that the employee's misconduct does not justify dismissal, the only remedy available is to award the employee damages for wrongful dismissal.

Termination of an employee's contract is justifiable on economic grounds where the employee's job has ceased to exist following a change in the economic situation or structure of the employer.

The procedure for dismissing an employee is highly formalistic. One should be aware that each of the various steps constituting this procedure must be followed scrupulously. If they are not, an employer may be subject to onerous sanctions.

The first step of the dismissal procedure involves sending a preliminary letter to the employee formally warning him of the employer's intention to dismiss him and inviting him to attend a preliminary meeting with the employer's representatives.

The second step involves the holding of a preliminary meeting between the employer and the employee at the offices of the company, at which the employee is orally informed of the employer's intention to dismiss him and the reasons for this dismissal. In the event that the employer persists in his intention to dismiss the employee after the preliminary meeting, he must send the employee formal notification of dismissal stating the reasons for it, and the date on which the dismissal becomes final which may not be before the expiration of any contractural notice period (*délai-congé*). In the event that the employer does not wish the employee to work during the relevant notice period, he must pay the employee compensation (*indemnité compensatrice de préavis*) equal to the amount of salary and fringe benefits including holiday benefits, which the employee would have earned had he continued to work during the notice period. The procedure is similar for a dismissal on economic grounds but in addition the employer must notify the director of the Employment Department of the dismissal.

In the case of a collective dismissal involving less than ten employees, the employer must consult the appropriate staff representatives concerning the proposed dismissals and provide any relevant information. The employer must comply with the dismissal procedure outlined above but in addition must give each employee he plans to dismiss the opportunity to enter into a retraining agreement (*convention de conversion*). The local Employment Department must be notified of such dismissals. However, since 6 July 1986 the prior approval of the Employment Department is no longer required.

In the case of a collective dismissal involving ten or more employees, the appropriate staff representatives must be consulted and the employer must provide any relevant information, as above. In addition the employer must outline the measures he intends to take to avoid or limit the dismissals and to facilitate the retraining of the employees who are to be dismissed. These must then be notified to the local Employment Department. The employer must also notify the latter of the collective dismissal.

As mentioned above, it is important for a potential employer to bear in mind that damages payable by an employer under French law to an employee who is dismissed may be substantial. French law permits the employer to negotiate a settlement (*transaction*) with the employee under which he and the employee agree on the amount of the termination payment to which the employee is entitled as a result of his dismissal. However, the settlement will be unenforceable if the termination payment negotiated is less than that required by law.

The law states that an employer must pay unfair dismissal damages (*indemnité de licenciement*) to any employee whom he has employed for two continuous years prior to his dismissal under an indefinite term contract. The only exception to such a rule is where a dismissal results from the gross or flagrant (*faute lourde*) misconduct of the employee. The severance pay is equal to one-tenth of the monthly salary for each year that the employee has worked for the employer (or 20 hours of his wages where the employee is paid by the hour) plus the *indemnité compensatrice de congés payés* in respect of holiday pay.

Where an employer dismisses an employee on a justifiable ground but fails to respect the dismissal procedures required by law (*licenciement irrégulier*), he may be ordered by the court to carry out such procedures and to pay damages representing a maximum of one month's salary to the employee.

Where an employer dismisses an employee without justifiable grounds, even if the correct dismissal procedures are followed (*licenciement abusif*), the court may suggest that the employee is reinstated (although as mentioned above he may not order it) and, in the case if either party refuses, may award, in favour of the employee, damages representing at least six months of his salary.

In addition *conventions collectives* may also include provisions allowing for the payment of unfair dismissal damages. However these will only be applicable to the extent that they are more favourable to the employee than the statutory minimum.

9.2.3 WORKING CONDITIONS

The statutory working week in France is 39 hours but in some industries such as the chemical industry it is less (38 hours). Recent legislation permits companies to negotiate more flexible working hours (up to 41–44 hours) per week without having to pay overtime or grant time off in compensation, on the condition that the annual average working week does not exceed 39 hours per week. The EC requires that minimum overtime payment be made for any hours worked in excess of the statutory working week:

—first 8 hours: 125 per cent of basic rates
—subsequent hours: 150 per cent of basic rates

Collective agreements often provide for further overtime payments where the employee works overtime at night, on Sundays or on national holidays. No employee may work more than 48 hours per week and the average number of hours worked per week over a twelve week period may not exceed 46 for any one individual. Furthermore, yearly overtime may not, in the absence of exceptional circumstances and with the prior authorisation of the Employment Department, exceed 130 hours per employee. French employment law also provides for time off in lieu in respect of overtime worked.

Except where the relevant collective bargaining agreement provides for more advantageous terms, employees in France are entitled to 2.5 working days holiday for each full month worked and thus, five weeks of vacation per year. For the purposes of calculating holiday entitlement a year runs from 1 June to 31 May.

9.2.4 WORKER REPRESENTATION

French employment law provides for three main categories of worker representation.

(1) Staff Representatives

Businesses employing more than eleven people must appoint staff representatives (*délegués du personnel*—DPs) these are elected for a one year period by the employees of the establishment. Their job is to present individual or collective complaints from the staff they represent to the employer, to ensure that all relevant *conventions collectives*, EC provisions and health and security regulations are complied with and to inform the government employment inspector of any breaches of these. DPs must meet with the employer at least once a month.

(2) The Workers Representation Committee

Presided over by the employer, the Workers Representation Committee (*Comité d'entreprise*—CE) is mandatory in a place of work establishment employing 50 persons or more. Representatives are elected to the committee and are consulted on all matters concerning the management and financial and economic development of the business including staff training and production methods. However they have no power of veto. They are responsible for the business's social and cultural activities (defined in the EC).

(3) Trade Unions

Where the number of employees of a business exceeds 50, trade union representatives may be appointed amongst the staff to represent their union before company management.

These and all other workers' representatives enjoy special protection against dismissal and other sanctions.

9.2.5 EMPLOYEE PROFIT SHARING SCHEMES

There are two types of profit sharing schemes in France. The first, known as *participation des salariés*, is mandatory for all businesses employing more than 100 employees for any six month period, whether consecutive or not during the course of a fiscal year. The employees may, but are not obliged to, join the scheme. The second kind of profit sharing plan, known as *intéressement des salariés*, is always voluntary.

An employer who adopts a profit sharing scheme must enter into an agreement known as *accord de participation* which either forms part of a collective bargaining agreement, negotiated with the appropriate union representatives or with the CE or proposed by the employer and approved by a majority vote of two-thirds of the employees.

A business which adopts a profit sharing scheme must credit, to a special reserve account each fiscal year, a statutorily imposed percentage of its net taxable French income. Each employee is, in principle, entitled to his *pro rata* share of such special reserve. The portion of the special reserve account to which an employee is entitled may not, as a general rule, be paid out or otherwise disposed of for a period of five years from the date on which the corresponding credit was made. All sums which a company credits to the special profit sharing reserve account are deductible for purposes of corporation tax.

An employer who wishes to set up the second scheme (*intéressement des salariés*) must enter into an *accord d'intéressement* with its staff. A major feature of the second scheme is that neither the employer nor the employee pay social security contributions on the amounts distributed. The amounts paid out are also deductible from the profits of the business. Each *accord* is different, since each is based upon a specific formula designed to measure the increased profitability of the business as worked out by the employer and its employees. However each is subject to the approval of the Employment Department and must be for a three year period at least. At the end of this period, the *accord* may be renewed, modified or cancelled.

9.2.6 SHARE OPTIONS

In 1970, the French Government enacted legislation to introduce share option schemes (*plan d'achat d'options*). This was reviewed in July 1984 to bring the French share option scheme closer to similar schemes in the USA. The main advantages offered by the scheme are as follows:

—the possibility of granting options at a reduced price;
—favourable tax treatment for businesses;
—low capital gains rate of 15 per cent on the disposal of shares.

It is also possible for companies quoted on the official French Stock Exchange or, under special circumstances, unquoted companies, to give their employees the opportunity to make a direct purchase of company stock subject to a holding period of five years. Companies may also sponsor saving investment plans (*plan d'épargne d'entreprise*) and employment investment funds (*fonds salariés*).

9.2.7 SOCIAL SECURITY SYSTEM

France has a mandatory national social security system covering major risks for all employees. The term social security covers five separate allowances: health (including maternity, incapacity and death), old age, family housing, occupational accident and illness. The system is financed by contributions from both employers and employees. Contributions paid by the employer are equal to approximately 45 per cent of the employee's gross salary.

9.3 MATERNITY LEAVE (*Congé de maternité*)

There is no statutory minimum period during which a woman must have worked before she is entitled to maternity leave under French employment legislation. The employee must send a medical certificate to her employer containing details of when the pregnancy began, the expected date of the birth etc in order to invoke her rights.

For the first two children a woman is entitled to 16 weeks

maternity leave which is usually split up as follows: six weeks before the birth and ten weeks after the birth, whilst for three or more children she is entitled to 26 weeks, eight weeks before and 18 weeks after.

During the maternity leave period a woman is entitled to social security benefits (usually equal to 80 per cent of her salary) calculated on a daily basis. An employer is not bound to pay the employee's salary during the maternity leave. However many *conventions collectives* provide that either all or part of the salary will continue to be paid. A woman's employment may not be terminated during the maternity period.

10
TAXATION

10.1 INTRODUCTION

The French tax system is both similar and different to its English equivalent. Accounts are prepared by accountants, in much the same way as in England although the profession is generally less creative in its approach due in part to the role of the auditor (*commissaire aux comptes*) who acts as a watchdog for the tax authorities.

However, the major difference is one of approach by the taxman. Whenever he decides upon an investigation, whether a simple one (*contrôle fiscale*) or a detailed one (*contrôle fiscale approfondie*), the experience is generally unforgettable. Its only close equivalent in England is a VAT inspection. One or more inspectors (*vérificateurs*) will descend like a wolf on the fold and life in the accounts department becomes difficult to say the least! Documents can be and frequently are impounded and taken away, an event which can have a dramatic effect on the day-to-day running of the business. The stylised way in which accounts have to be kept (with each page of journals stamped and numbered by the clerk of the Commercial Court preventing the removal of pages) is another substantial difference. Equally, vouchers need to be kept punctiliously or deductions will be refused. Having said that, in the absence of fraud there is a limitation period on back tax of only three years.

The best advice one can give is never to file an oddball return. As long as things proceed in a consistent way the likelihood of problems is limited. There is also said to be an advantage in having one's registered office in the eighth *arrondissement* of Paris, since there are so many companies registered there that it is difficult for the available staff to be as exacting as they might otherwise be.

10.2 VALUE ADDED TAX (*taxe sur la valeur ajoutée*)

Value added tax (*TVA*) is the most important form of French indirect taxation. Broadly speaking it is a tax on general consumption which, in theory, hits all goods consumed (whether they are manufactured abroad or not) and services performed in France. Its ambit is wide—it covers all business activities carried on by taxable entities. This includes not only industrial, commercial and agricultural activities, but also professional services and other activities which are classified as civil. The latter category now includes lawyers following the passing of a recent law. There is no minimum threshold for business turnover.

Certain insurance, banking and financial activities and those carried on by non-profit making associations are however exempt. Similarly, although the import of goods into France gives rise to TVA, exports do not.

Transactions involving the sale of certain types of property are subject to property TVA and are subject to special rules relating to credits, methods of rates and imposition.

In theory each taxable entity is responsible for collecting, from its customers TVA payable on the sale of taxable goods or the provision of taxable services and handing it over to the tax authorities. TVA is a non-cumulative tax and is only levied on the value of the services performed or the value added to goods sold. Under certain circumstances a taxable entity may set off the TVA it collects against the tax it owes for a particular taxable period. This is, of course, very similar to the situation in England.

The standard rate for TVA is 18.6 per cent. However, a number of different rates apply to specific goods and services, among them:

(i) Medicines paid for by social security; 2.1 per cent
(ii) Food products, books, public transport, letting of furnished property; 5.5 per cent
(iii) Cars, photographic equipment, perfumes. 25 per cent

10.3 BUSINESS TAXATION

10.3.1 DIRECT BUSINESS TAXATION

As a general rule French corporation tax (*impôt sur les sociétés*) is levied on profits made by the *société de capitaux* (see

Chapter 3) eg *société anonyme, société en commandite par actions* or companies with commercial objects eg *société à responsabilité limitée*.

However a company carrying on civil activities (*société civile*) such as the holding of property can become liable to corporation tax if its 'commercial' income (ie income arising from a commercial activity such as the habitual letting of property) exceeds on average ten per cent of their total income.

Similarly *sociétés* which are not *sociétés de capitaux* but are considered by their nature to be commercial such as *société en nom collectif* and *société en commandite simple* may also be subject to corporation tax in certain circumstances although they are normally regarded as fiscally transparent.

On the other hand, certain types of *société de personnes* which have a corporate structure are nevertheless regarded as fiscally transparent for tax purposes. Therefore they are treated similarly to English partnerships ie the *associé*'s share of profits corresponding to his 'partnership share' in the company are aggregated with his global income for income tax purposes. Similarly, each partner may deduct his *pro rata* share of the partnership's losses from his taxable income. For this reason, these types of company are often used as vehicles in company group structures. French companies which are fiscally transparent for tax purposes are: *sociétés civiles, sociétés en participation, sociétés à responsabilité de caractère familiale, entreprises unipersonnelles à responsabilité limitée* (EURL), *groupements d'intérêt économique, groupements d'intérêt public, sociétés immobilières transparentes, sociétés civiles professionnelles, sociétés de copropriété de navire, sociétés civiles de moyens, groupements forestiers, groupements agricoles, syndicats mixte de gestion forestière*.

10.3.2 TAX INCENTIVES

Certain types of companies set up to carry out particular activities benefit from certain tax incentives eg *société d'investissement à capital variable* (SICAV), *société immobilière pour le commerce et l'industrie* (SICOMI), *société immobilière d'investissement*.

New companies also benefit from tax incentives, thus, companies created after 1 October 1988 to carry on new industrial or commercial activities are exempt from corporation tax or income tax as appropriate during the first two years of their operation and exempt from tax on 75 per cent, 50 per cent, and 25 per cent respectively of their profits over the following three years. The exemption is only available if at least 50 per cent of the voting rights in the new company are held by individuals, rather than other companies. Companies created since 1 October 1988 to rescue an industrial company in financial difficulties are exempt from corporation tax and the annual minimum tax (*imposition forfaitaire annuelle des sociétés*) for two years following their creation.

Incentives are also available to the foreign subsidiary of a French company which is set up with the aim of selling goods manufactured in France. These incentives differ according to whether the subsidiary is established in an EEC country or a non-EEC country. Where a parent company owns at least 50 per cent of an EEC subsidiary, the parent company can transfer to a tax-free reserve an amount of its own profits equivalent to the losses incurred by the subsidiary in the first five years of the subsidiary's operations up to the amount it has invested in the subsidiary. The reserve is recaptured as the subsidiary becomes profitable, and in any event at the end of the tenth year of operations. When the subsidiary is established in a non-EEC country, the parent company must own at least 25 per cent of the subsidiary, the transfers to the tax-free reserve are equivalent to the amounts invested by the parent, and recapture takes place in equal instalments over the six to ten year period.

Investors in the *Départements d'Outre Mer* (DOM) may qualify for participation in several investment incentive schemes offering various tax savings (*Loi Pons*). The most important of these are the 33.3 per cent reduction of taxable income available to companies engaged in specified activities, and the ability to deduct 100 per cent of a company's investment in various sectors eg industry, tourism, transport, fishing, public works etc with the prior consent of the French tax authorities in certain cases. Certain investments in the TOM also qualify for tax relief. These particular reliefs could, and arguably should, have made the DOM/TOM into an internal tax haven, but to date this has not happened.

10.3.3 INDIRECT BUSINESS TAXATION

In addition to indirect taxes which are not covered in this book, France has the following registration taxes (*droits d'enregistrement*):

(i) The initial subscription of share capital on the formation of a company attracts a registration tax of one per cent on cash contributions up to a fixed maximum of FF 430. No tax is payable on additional subscriptions to the capital of the company.

(ii) Capitalisations of earnings in corporation tax paying companies in the form of a stock dividend or bonus issue of shares attract a duty of three per cent.

(iii) Share transfers are subject to a registration tax of 4.8 per cent. But the transfer of shares in an SA (*actions*) is normally not subject to such registration tax unless the transfer is contained in a written agreement (which it does not have to be). Since 1 January 1991 registration tax has been reduced to one per cent on share transfer documents (*actes portant cession d'actions*).

(iv) On the liquidation of a company, the distribution of its assets attracts a registration tax of one per cent.

(v) A transfer of land normally attracts a tax of 16.6 per cent but this is reduced to 5.4 per cent for dwelling houses. In addition, regional taxes of about 1.15 per cent to 1.6 per cent are payable. Transfers of buildings that are less than five years old are subject to *TVA* instead of these taxes.

(vi) A sale of Goodwill (*fonds de commerce*) is subject to registration tax at rates of up to 14.2 per cent.

(vii) Contributions in kind such as real estate or Goodwill are also subject to registration tax. The law provides for the application of two different rates, depending upon the relevant circumstances:
—one per cent of the value of the contribution made by an individual for the benefit of a company which is not subject to corporation tax;
—one per cent of the value of the contribution made by a company which is subject to corporation tax for the benefit of a company which is similarly subject to income tax;
—11.4 per cent of the value of the contribution made by an individual or by a company not subject to corporation tax for the benefit of a company which is subject to corporation tax and vice versa.

10.4 DEFINITION OF CORPORATE PROFIT

Unlike French income tax, the French corporation tax system is essentially levied on French territory, the relevant company being assessed on profits arising from carrying on a trade or business in France. Profits or losses of a business carried on outside France are not taken into account. Taxable profits are based on the difference between net assets at the beginning and end of the year as shown in the company accounts, or on the profits disclosed therein. Expenditure incurred for business purposes is deductible unless it is of a capital nature. Gains on fixed assets are included in taxable income. They are divided into short-term and long-term gains:
—Short-term capital gains are gains on transfers of assets held for less than two years including the portion of gains due to the depreciation claimed on depreciable assets held for two years or more.
—Long-term capital gains are gains on transfers of assets held for two years or more, to the extent that they are not attributable to depreciation previously charged against profits.
Short-term gains are included in operating profits and are taxed

at the ordinary rate. Long-term gains are aggregated separately and are subject to a lower tax rate of 19 per cent (15 per cent on intellectual property and 25 per cent on building sites) provided the net tax is not distributed and credited to a special reserve account on the debit side of the balance sheet in the books of the company.

Dividends received by a company as a general rule are included in the parent's taxable income, with the benefit of a tax credit (*avoir fiscal*) on domestic dividends or any withholding tax paid on foreign dividends.

However, a company holding more than ten per cent of a subsidiary (whether French or foreign) can exclude distributions received (with the exception of a five per cent service charge) from its taxable income. This affiliation privilege is highly beneficial and probably more generous than in any other EEC country. If the subsidiary is in a country which France considers to be a tax haven (which for these purposes means where tax rates are less than two-thirds French ones) the business of the subsidiary must be predominantly in the local market (TC art 209B). This effectively excludes the possibility of taking profits artificially off-shore.

Losses can be carried forward for five years. However, the carry forward of losses attributable to depreciation has no time limit. Losses may be carried back for three years if certain conditions are fulfilled. In general, profits and losses from foreign sources are not taken into account for the computation of the taxable income of French resident companies.

An advance corporation tax (*précompte*) is due on the distribution of profits. Foreign dividends, other than those distributed by a subsidiary, are taxed in full unless exempt under a double taxation treaty.

10.5 DIRECT PERSONAL TAX

Individuals are classified as either resident or non-resident. Residents of France are subject to a national income tax on their worldwide income. An individual is resident if either his main residence is in France, if he carries on professional activities in the country or if it is his centre of economic interest. A foreign individual resident in France is similarly taxable on his worldwide income (subject to any tax treaty).

A non-resident foreign individual pays French tax only on income from French sources or, if he has a house in France, on three times its rental value, whichever is the higher, if he is not otherwise a taxpayer and the property is not rented and tax paid on the rent. EEC residents are exempted from this charge.

Income taxable in the hands of an individual is divided into seven schedules:

(i) Property income;
(ii) Industrial and commercial income—this covers professional, commercial and artisanal income. In addition, *associés* of fiscally transparent companies, which undertake commercial, industrial, artisanal or mining activities are taxable under this schedule in respect of their shares of the company profits unless they are themselves companies subject to corporation tax;
(iii) Certain directors' remuneration;
(iv) Agricultural income;
(v) Wages, salaries, pensions and life annuities;
(vi) Non-commercial income;
(vii) Investment income.

In addition, short-term capital gains are assessed as ordinary income.

Exemption from French tax is granted under all tax treaties to residents of signatory countries working in France for less than 183 days in one tax year provided that the employer is a resident of the signatory country, also that the employee's remuneration is not ultimately borne by a permanent establishment in France.

A self-employed individual is taxed on a preceding year basis on his global income without being able to shelter his profits in reserves in the way that a company is able to do. Similarly, the *associé* of a fiscally transparent company will be taxed immediately on his *pro rata* share of the company income. French residents are subject to sliding scale tax rates ranging from 0 to

58.6 per cent (on 1990 income). However, certain tax reliefs are available in order to reduce taxable income thus ensuring a more moderate average rate of taxation.

Where a self-employed person or sole trader has his accounts maintained by an approved management centre (*centre de gestion agréé*), he is permitted to claim, when computing his taxable income, a 20 per cent deduction on the first FF 413,200 of his income and ten per cent deduction on the slice of his income between FF 413,200 and FF 558,000. This deduction is equivalent to those allowed in respect of salaries. Social security and some pension contributions, alimony and payments for the support of parents and gifts to charities (within limits) are also deductible. A tax credit is granted for certain life insurance premiums and for certain interest on house purchase loans for a principal residence.

The family quota (*quotient familial*) system mitigates the effects of the sliding scale tax rate. The taxable income of the family is divided by the number of family parts/units, the sliding scale is applied to determine the rate and this rate is then applied to total income.

10.6 Transfer pricing

The tax authorities may impute constructive income to a French company if the latter directly or indirectly transfers income to a foreign enterprise by means of a transaction which is not at arm's length in circumstances where both companies are under the same control and, if the foreign enterprise is established in a tax haven, joint control is not required. Other anti-avoidance provisions seek to prevent the hidden transfers of profits, otherwise taxable in France, out of the jurisdiction. The French tax authorities have a very robust attitude to avoidance schemes which is reinforced by the highly formalistic way in which accounts need to be kept and the independent role of the French auditor (*commissaire aux comptes*). There is an overriding provision of French tax procedure (art 67 *Livre de Procédure Fiscale*) which seeks to unwind any scheme or arrangement whose sole or main purpose is either to obtain tax benefits or is otherwise wholly tax-driven. Whilst this is very disturbing, actions brought under this section alleging *abus de droit* are extremely rare. Equally, if proper care is taken in structuring deals which have an objectively justifiable purpose, the risks in France are no greater than in the United Kingdom.

11
INSOLVENCY

11.1 INTRODUCTION

It is a sad fact of commercial life in the 1990s that one of the most important considerations to which anyone doing business anywhere must have regard is the question of insolvency, either his own or of those with whom he is in a business relationship. The law on the subject in France has been substantially redrawn by the Law of 1 March 1984 and of 25 January 1985 ('the New Laws') which are themselves an amended and extended redraft of the Law of 13 July 1967 ('the Old Law'). No useful purpose will be served by dealing in any detail with the old Law. Suffice to say that it was not seen as a successful attempt to help companies avoid insolvent liquidation which was in substantial part its rationale. Furthermore, prior to 31 December 1989 French law did not grant any relief to private individuals who became insolvent. The law of that date goes some way to granting relief but it is not as extensive as its English counterpart. Personal insolvency in France remains a harrowing experience and a long lasting impediment.

For anyone used to Anglo-Saxon notions of insolvency, the new laws on the matter have many similarities to their Anglo-Saxon counterparts and indeed are, in part, inspired by them. However, the consequences of insolvency in France in a business context are generally even more worrying than in England. The judge dealing with the matter has far-reaching powers and discretions not all of which are subject to the normal appeals procedure. Equally, and France has a long history in this area, the circumstances in which managers of a business may be called to account to its creditors are not only in theory wider than in England but also more regularly applied. If one is a creditor this is encouraging, but if one is a manager of an insolvent business it can be very distressing. Outside the scope of members of a supervisory board in a two-tier SA structure, France has no notion of non-executive directors and it may be difficult to avoid joint and several liability with co-directors, even if no active part in the running of a business has been taken. The watchword is caution and proper legal advice must be taken sooner rather than later if problems are to be avoided or attenuated. Fraud is a frequent allegation in French court proceedings and French counsel has much less reticence about pleading it. Even bad faith on its own may be sufficient to cause substantial embarrassment or even liability. There can be few other areas where timely legal advice can be as valuable as in relation to insolvency issues.

11.2 BUSINESS INSOLVENCY

As in many European jurisdictions, bankruptcy law in France is codified. As mentioned above the old law did not achieve its objective of rescuing firms which were in difficulty. The old law was criticised mainly because insolvency proceedings were a disaster for creditors. The majority of the proceedings ended in liquidation and not rehabilitation as had been hoped. The proceedings were slow and complicated, employees' interests were often ignored, and there was no machinery for consultation.

As the economic crisis deepened, increasing the frequency of corporate insolvency, legislation had to be reviewed in order to be adapted to economic and social realities. The reform was split in two different steps which correspond to two levels of difficulty which a business may encounter.

On the one hand, the Law of 1 March 1984 (*Prévention et règlement amiable des difficultés des entreprises*) deals with a series of measures designed to prevent the insolvency and to organise an agreement between the enterprise and its major creditors.

On the other hand, the Law of 25 January 1985 (*Redressement et liquidation judiciaire des entreprises*) seeks to succeed where the previous legislation failed, that is to say in rehabilitating the business. As with the old law the new laws require considerable involvement of the court and are therefore quite formal. In order to achieve its purpose, the law provides a single step which initiates a process similar to an administration order in England (*jugement d'ouverture d'une procédure de redressement judiciaire*).

After a period of observation and enquiry, the court decides whether the business can survive (with or without sale of some of its assets) or if not orders a winding-up (*liquidation judiciaire*). If rehabilitation is deemed feasible an official is appointed to carry out the proposal (*commissaire à l'exécution du plan*).

The new laws split the profession of insolvency practitioner which was previously carried on by a single profession known as the *Syndic*. As a result, the management functions of the business are now carried on by an administrator (*administrateur*) appointed by the court during the rehabilitation period.

The creditors who were previously grouped together in a *masse des créanciers* are now represented by a creditors' representative (*représentant des créanciers*). Any liquidation is carried out by a liquidator (*liquidateur*) who is also appointed by the Court. The new laws increased the role of the employees who are now often consulted during the proceedings and offered some protection.

Under the New Laws a simplified procedure has been introduced for all businesses with 50 employees or less and an annual turnover of less than FF 20 million. This simplified procedure applies to more than 90 per cent of all insolvent businesses. The main difference between the two procedures is that under the former, the observation period is shorter than under the latter and the appointment of an administrator is not mandatory.

As far as the manager's liability for the debts of a business is concerned, liability may only be imposed where an error of management has been proved. Thus, the burden of proof has been reversed and management is no longer required to prove as a positive that it acted prudently as used to be required under the Old Law. Many of the sanctions imposed for acts of mismanagement under the New Laws have been decriminalised and consequently, some acts which were previously criminal offences become civil offences. However in practice the Court has considerable discretion to find managers liable as the Court interprets strictly the standards of business procedure which management should display.

For creditors, it should be noted that the priority of security interests such as mortgages may be disturbed since preferential rights are given to certain types of creditors, particularly during the rehabilitation period.

11.3 MEASURES INTENDED TO PREVENT INSOLVENCY

These measures are regulated by the Law of 1 March 1984.

11.3.1 AMBER LIGHT PROCEEDINGS (*Procédure d'alerte*)

This court procedure concerns commercial companies organised with a capital base where their financial statements show a net loss greater than one-third of the equity of such company. In this case, the President of the Commercial Court may issue a summons ordering the management to appear before him and to explain the measures that will be taken to improve the financial situation.

Requests for information about the operation of the company may be made by the statutory auditor (*commissaire aux comptes*) and the Workers Representation Committee (*comité d'entreprise*) of the company.

11.3.2 MORATORIA

Whenever the draft financial statements of a business indicate financial difficulties which cannot be covered by way of a loan on normal commercial terms, the management may file a written petition with the Commercial Court or Superior Court (*tribunal de grande instance*) (if the object of the company is not commercial) requesting the appointment of a conciliator (*conciliateur*).

Such a petition must describe the financial difficulties of the company, the financial methods envisaged to rehabilitate it and the terms of debt rescheduling and/or retirement which could permit the company to implement such methods. The conciliator's role is to assist the business in negotiating an agreement between the company and its major creditors in order to reschedule or retire the company's debts. Such proceedings are confidential. If an agreement is reached it has to be filed with the clerk of the court, the public prosecutor and the *Commissaire de la République* (formerly the *préfet* of a district). Such agreement bars any action by creditors who are a party to the agreement as long as it is observed by the business.

If the business fails to observe its obligations, winding-up proceedings may be commenced against it forthwith.

11.4 REHABILITATION

There is a simple procedure under the new laws for seeking the protection of the court which may or may not end in a winding-up. English law distinctions between members' and creditors' proceedings are not relevant.

11.4.1 INITIATION OF PROCEEDINGS

The new laws apply to traders, artisans, farmers or any private entities which have a legal personality and which cannot satisfy their financial obligations. This inability is known in France as *cessation des paiements*. A French business is considered to be in *cessation des paiements* where its liquid assets are insufficient to pay its debts as they fall due. This is the same test as in England. Any business in such a situation must, within 15 days, petition the appropriate court (*tribunal de commerce, tribunal de grande instance*) as the case may be for a rehabilitation order. The business must file a statement of its financial situation with the court; this operation is known in France as *le dépôt de bilan*.

In common usage a business failure is often characterised by this term, which is incorrect as the business may still be rehabilitated. The rehabilitation proceedings may be brought by the business itself. They may also be brought by the Court of its own motion at the request of the public prosecutor or upon the petition of one or more business creditors either where the latter are unpaid or where the business has failed to comply with a *moratorium* agreement (see **11.3.2**).

A creditor's petition (*assignation*) must specify the nature and the amount of any claims and must indicate all action already undertaken to recover them. Thus a creditor's petition must be justified and based upon proper evidence. If it is not the creditor may be liable to the business for *abus de droit*. The court hears the management of the business and the representatives of the Workers Representative Committee (if any) and any other person considered necessary. The business is officially in rehabilitation once the court makes a rehabilitation order.

As required by statute, the court determines in its rehabilitation order the date on which the business effectively became unable to pay its debts (*cessation des paiements*). This date is very important as the period from this date until the date of the rehabilitation order is characterised as a fraudulent preference period (*période suspecte*). Payments made or commitments entered into during this period, such as finance on economically unfair terms, may be declared null and void by the court. Nevertheless, the date of the *cessation des paiements* may never be more than 18 months before the date of the rehabilitation order. The rehabilitation order may be appealed to the Court of Appeal and thereafter to the Supreme Court (*Cour de Cassation*) by the business, the creditor must file the petition or the public prosecutor within ten days of the drawing up of the order.

11.4.2 PARTICIPANTS IN REHABILITATION PROCEEDINGS

(1) The court

The powers of the court have been increased by the New Laws. The court adopts the most appropriate measures such as:
—redundancies;
—the cessation of a type of business;
—the imposition on creditors of uniform payments;
—the continuation of the business;
—the transfer of all or part of the business to third parties on terms decided by the court;
—or liquidation.

(2) The *juge commissaire*

The *juge commissaire* is chosen from the available judges on the local bench. He is the 'anchorman' of the proceedings. He supervises any administrator and the creditors' representative. He reports to the court about all disputes arising in the proceedings before such disputes are heard before the court. Such a report is mandatory since a judgment given without it may be declared null and void. The *juge commissaire* rules by 'ordinance' (*ordonnance*) on matters which are subject to his jurisdiction such as the proof or the rejection of creditors' claims. Such ordinances are subject to an appeal to the Court of Appeal.

(3) Public prosecutor

The public prosecutor is kept regularly informed by the administrator and/or the creditors' representative about the proceedings. He may require a special extension of the observation period for no more than six months. During such period, the public prosecutor may authorise a contract of lease management (*location-gérance*) (see Chapter 4).

(4) Insolvency practitioners

The profession of insolvency practitioner has been split in two: the administrators (*administrateurs*) on the one hand and the creditors' representatives (*représentants des créanciers*) on the other hand.

  (i) The administrator

The administrator represents the interests of the business. His powers are fixed by the court. He may be charged with:

—supervising the management of the business;

—assisting in the management of the business.

The appointment of an administrator is not mandatory under the simplified procedure. The administrator has a very important role in the proceedings since he is responsible for preparing a report on the economic and social situation of the business (*bilan économique et social*). In such a report, he will either propose a plan of rehabilitation or winding-up. Since an administrator is the agent of the business, he will be liable to the proprietors of it if he is negligent in his duties and they suffer as a result.

(ii) The creditors' representative

A creditors' representative is always appointed. He acts on behalf of and in the interest of the creditors. All creditors must file their claims with the creditors' representative, who verifies them. If the court decides on winding-up, the creditors' representative becomes the liquidator (*liquidateur*).

(5) Employees' representative

An employees' representative is chosen from among the employees of the business to check the list of employees' claims which are established by the creditors' representative. The employees' representative is also heard on many issues affecting the interests of the employees generally and serves as a channel of communication to the workforce during the rehabilitation period.

(6) *Contrôleurs et experts*

In addition one or more *contrôleurs* may be appointed to assist both the creditors' representative and the *juge commissaire*. An *expert en diagnostic* may be appointed to assist the administrator in preparation of the *bilan économique et social*.

11.4.3 THE DIFFERENT STEPS IN THE REHABILITATION PROCEEDINGS

(1) The rehabilitation period

The rehabilitation period normally lasts for six months which is renewable once for an additional six month period. Under the simplified procedure, this period consists of an initial investigation period not exceeding 30 days followed by a further four month period. The period may be terminated by the court at any time at the request of the administrator, the creditors' representative, public prosecutor or the business itself, if there is no real chance of rehabilitation. The court could make a liquidation order on the same day as a rehabilitation order but the Supreme Court has held (Cass. Civ. Comm. 4 November 1986) that a rehabilitation period must be ordered beforehand, even if it is only for one day.

During this period, as we have seen, a report on the economic and employment situation of the debtor (*bilan économique et social*) and a plan of rehabilitation, if such rehabilitation seems possible, must be prepared by the administrator, assisted by the management of the business and one or more experts if necessary.

If such a plan of rehabilitation is prepared, the administrator drafts proposals pursuant to which the creditors are invited to agree to waive and/or postpone the payment of their claims. These proposals are sent to the creditors' representative who, after consultation, has to make a return of the replies he has received from the creditors.

During the rehabilitation period, third parties may submit to the administrator, offers to purchase one or more sectors of the business or the whole of the business. The offers and the documents attached thereto are filed with the clerk of the court who sends these to the *juge-commissaire*, the management and shareholders (if any) of the business. Such offers are firm and irrevocable once the administrator's report has been filed and until the court has ruled on the proposed plan. The court must rule within one month of the filing of the report.

Since the scope of the new laws is essentially the

rehabilitation of the business, it is necessary for its survival that former management continues to manage during the rehabilitation period, unless the court orders the administrator to run the company himself. This it will do if the management has proved itself clearly incompetent. The court may order the removal of some or all of the management.

Unauthorised managerial acts performed by managers, however, remain valid as far as third parties are concerned, provided they contracted in good faith.

Nevertheless, under both the ordinary and simplified procedures, the management is supervised and therefore, all purchases of property other than in the ordinary course of business, the granting of all mortgages or guarantees and all settlements of claims must receive the prior written approval of the *juge commissaire*.

Some acts are simply prohibited such as any payment of debts incurred before the date of the rehabilitation order. Contracts existing at that time may be enforced either by the administrator or the business. The mere fact of the making of the order does not relieve the contracting parties of their obligation to perform, even if the business was in breach at that date. However, the administrator must fulfil the contractual obligations which arise during the rehabilitation period.

If the administrator decides to disclaim outstanding contracts, the other party is entitled to damages for breach of the contract under the general law of contracts. Such damages will, however, be considered as unsecured debts which would have to be declared to the creditors' representative and rank *pari passu* with other similar claims.

A party to a contract with a company in rehabilitation may require the administrator to affirm or disclaim the contract by notice served by *huissier*, or return receipt requested registered mail. If he fails to reply affirmatively within one month of receipt of such a request, he is deemed to disclaim.

All actions concerning the enforcement of claims which arose prior to the rehabilitation order are stayed. All creditors of the business, except employees, must file their proof of claims with the creditors' representative within two months of the publication of the rehabilitation order in *BODACC*. This time limit must be strictly observed under pain of exclusion of the claim.

However, if a creditor fails to file his proof within this period he may petition the court. Such an action is known as *action en rèleve de forclusion* which seeks authority to prove his claim outside the time limit. However, it must be brought within one year of the original order and the failure to prove must be justified by serious reasons.

The claims are checked by the creditors' representative and submitted to the *juge commissaire* for admission or rejection. A decision of the *juge commissaire* may be appealed to the Court of Appeal within ten days following the official notification to the claimant.

The new laws and specifically art 40 of the Law of 25 January 1985 has created a new category of creditors namely those who become creditors of the business after the rehabilitation order. Such creditors are preferred and so do not need to file their claims with the creditors' representative.

During the rehabilitation period, employees may be made redundant for economic reasons provided it is urgent, inevitable and necessary. Such redundancies require prior authorisation by the *juge commissaire* after consultation by the administrator of the workers committee (*comité d'entreprise*) (if any) or the employees' representatives.

(2) The judgment period

The administrator files his report and any proposed plan with the clerk of the court at least eight days before the expiry of the rehabilitation period. The Court must publish its decision before the expiry of the rehabilitation period.

(3) Options in the proceedings
   (i) Rehabilitation

The court may decide to order the rehabilitation of the business. Prior to such a decision, the court may hear representations by the business as well as the employees' and creditors' representatives. Unlike the situation under the old law which required the plan of rehabilitation to have been approved by a certain percentage of the creditors, the new laws allow the court to adopt the rehabilitation plan even if the business, the creditors' representative or the employees' representative object to it. The plan adopted by the court may call for one of the three following solutions:

—the continuation of the business;
—the continuation of the business including the disposal of one or more autonomous sectors of the business (partial transfer); or
—the total transfer of the business.

The court may subordinate its decision to approve the rehabilitation to the removal of one or more managers of the business. The shares of the managers may be declared untransferable. Alternatively, the court may order the compulsory transfer of their shares. The execution of the rehabilitation proposal is supervised by a *commissaire à l'exécution du plan* appointed by the court who is often the former *administrateur*.

   (ii) Liquidation

If the court decides on liquidation (*liquidation judiciaire*), all debts become due and payable. The liquidator converts assets into cash and distributes such cash among the creditors according to the law on their respective priorities.

11.5 RIGHTS OF CREDITORS

Although any creditor may petition the appropriate court in order to obtain a rehabilitation order, the New Laws are hard on creditors and especially on those with mortgages. During the rehabilitation period, creditors' rights are frozen. Although a rehabilitation plan may be appealed against by the creditors' representative within ten days, a disposal plan may not be appealed at all. Where a rehabilitation plan is ordered, the court may impose on the creditors specific terms of payment. Pursuant to art 40 of the Law of 25 January 1985 some creditors have, in any event, preferential rights as follows:

(i) remuneration due to employees in respect of their last sixty days salary;
(ii) Court and administrative expenses;
(iii) commercial loans and claims arising on contracts continued by the administrator during the rehabilitation period;
(iv) wages and salaries of staff during the rehabilitation period.

An employer in France is required by the EC art L 143.11.1 to insure payment of a proportion of his employees' salary and in principle this insurance is available for the benefit of employees in the proceedings. Preferential creditors are known as *créanciers privilégiés*.

French law governing security interests makes a distinction between general privilege (*privilèges généraux*) and special privilege (*privilèges spéciaux*). General privilege only applies to personal property (*biens meubles*) and charges on real property (*hypothèques*) which must be registered in the Mortgage Registry (*conservation des hypothèques*) to be valid against third parties. However, the general privilege of the French tax authorities and Social Security department may be readily converted into a legal charge on any real property and such a charge has to be registered. Three heads of general privilege affect personal property as well as real property:

(i) Court costs;
(ii) Employees' privileges and rights;
(iii) Those of authors, artists and composers.

As a general rule, creditors with a special privilege secured by charge (*nantissement*) or a mortgage are overreached by art 40 rights, by employees' privilege and Court costs privilege. The only interests which defeat such claims is a pledge with retention of goods (*gage avec droit de retention*), retention of title clause (*clause de réserve de propriété*) or rights arising under a finance lease of capital goods used for business purposes.

Such interests permit the beneficiary to claim (*revendiquer*) the goods which belong to him. Such an action is known as an *action de revendication* and is similar to a replevin action. In all of these three cases a successful action will lead to the restitution of the goods. An action must be commenced within three months of the initial rehabilitation order. Any money claim will have to prove in the liquidation, although the administrator or any liquidator may purge the first two claims, but not the third, by payment of any price due.

The lessor under a finance lease (*crédit bail*) should claim even if the lease is continued by the administrator, since case law is not very clear as to whether such continuation is binding. Retention of title is governed by the Law of 12 May 1980 and art 121.2 of the Law of 25 January 1985. A retention clause must be in writing in a document executed no later than the date of delivery of the goods. The goods concerned may not be fungibles or raw materials and must be identifiable at the date of the action.

In the event that the goods in suit were sold by the business to a third party, the claimant cannot claim the property if the third party acted in good faith (art 2279 Civil Code). He may only claim the resale price as an unsecured claim. There is no equivalent here to the 'Nemo Dat' rule and no tracing action is possible.

11.5.1 RESPONSIBILITIES AND LIABILITIES OF THE MANAGEMENT OF AN INSOLVENT BUSINESS

French law extends the sanctions which may be applied to managers of a business which are liable for negligent management to those on whose instructions they habitually act known as 'managers in fact' (*gérants de fait*). A manager may be required to make up, in whole or in part, any deficit arising on a liquidation if he has committed errors in management that lead to the deficit. Such an error must be proved by the plaintiff as well as the causal connection with the liquidation. This procedure may be started by the administrator, the creditors' representative, the *juge commissaire* or the public prosecutor. Three years after a rehabilitation or the liquidation order such claims become time-barred.

By virtue of art 182 of the 1985 Law, the Court may also 'extend' a rehabilitation order to one or more managers of the business (*extension de redressement judiciaire*) if:

(i) he has used company assets as his own;
(ii) he has engaged in trade activities in his personal interest, under the cover of the business;
(iii) he has made use of the assets or the credit of the business in a way adversely affecting its interests, or with a view to favouring another business in which he holds a direct or indirect interest;
(iv) he continued the business to further his own interest where such continuation could only lead to the insolvency of the business;
(v) he falsified the accounts of the business, failed to keep books up to proper accounting standards or caused the disappearance of the books of the business;
(vi) he fraudulently increased the liabilities of the business or misappropriated corporate assets.

The manager must contribute to the losses of the business to the extent determined by the Court.

The court may also make an order of personal bankruptcy (*faillite personnelle*) against any individual concerned. This is not like a Receiving Order but rather a bar to further trading activities and may include *inter alia*:

(i) a prohibition against undertaking or controlling indirectly or directly any business activities;
(ii) a prohibition against using his voting rights in the business;

(iii) an obligation to transfer his share of the business.

The court may make such an order in several situations including those set out in art 8(2) and in the following additional situations:

(i) where the manager procured funds on commercially imprudent terms in order to delay filing for insolvency protection;

(ii) where the manager engaged in deals which were disproportionate to the capacity of the enterprise according to its financial situation;

(iii) where the manager consciously made preferential payment to some creditors to the prejudice of others, after the date on which the business could no longer make current payments;

(iv) where the manager failed to file for insolvency protection within 15 days of knowing or being deemed to know that it could no longer trade.

The duration of these sanctions is fixed by the court in its order but cannot be for less than five years.

Managers may also be subject to criminal penalties (*banqueroute*). Thus, fraudulent misappropriation of corporate assets, fraudulent increase of corporate liabilities, fictitious or irregular book-keeping, or borrowing on imprudent terms, are punishable by imprisonment for three months to five years, and by a fine of between FF 10,000 to FF 200,000. The same category of penalties applies to:

—any person who files fictitious proofs of debt in a winding-up or conceals business assets;

—managers who conceal personal assets in bad faith in order to protect them from a possible court order to make up the losses of a business.

The judge in criminal proceedings may also impose the civil sanctions referred to above.

11.6 PERSONAL INSOLVENCY

The Law of 31 December 1989 introduced for individuals in France a measure of insolvency protection. It contains two different procedures which complement each other and which are similar to those stipulated by the new laws for businesses.

Firstly, the *'règlement amiable'* is an agreement which must receive the approbation of the debtor and his major creditors in order to solve the debtor's financial problems. This procedure is appropriate where an individual in good faith cannot face all his personal (ie non-business) accruing and due debts. The debtor is said to be in a situation of *surendettement*. This procedure is dealt with by an administrative commission which exists in each *département* and is initiated by the debtor.

The administrative commission tries to conciliate all parties and agree to a scheme of arrangement which could reschedule or retire some or all of the debtor's debts. The administrative commission, if successful, informs the judge of the *tribunal d'instance* of the debtor's home address, which has exclusive jurisdiction in the matter, of the matters contained in the scheme entered into by the debtor and his major creditors.

Secondly, a 'bankruptcy order' may be made by the *tribunal d'instance* of the debtor's home address. Such tribunals are competent for minor civil cases and have similar jurisdiction to the County Court. As for the previous proceeding, the debtor must in good faith be unable to meet his personal debts as they fall due.

This procedure may be commenced by the debtor, the *tribunal d'instance*, or on the request of another judge. It may also be commenced if the administrative procedure has failed or if, by the time a scheme is agreed, a creditor has commenced or maintains enforcement proceedings, since the administrative procedure does not automatically stay such actions.

Under this procedure the judge of the *tribunal d'instance* has greater powers than those usually conferred to him by art 1244 of the Civil Code to grant relief for debt. He may decide to:

(i) suspend any enforcement proceedings temporarily;
(ii) reschedule the payment of part of the debts provided they are not debts owed to the tax authorities;
(iii) provide for payment of principal only on debts or for interest only;

(iv) reduce the rate of interest payable on debts outstanding.

This procedure does not, of course, apply to any trading or business activities.

12
FINANCING A FRENCH COMPANY

12.1 INTRODUCTION

The various ways in which a French commercial undertaking can obtain finance are very similar to those available in the United Kingdom and the categories into which they are divided in this respect will be familiar. The major area of substantial difference relates to cheques. In common with most Latin countries the whole business of cheques is fraught with difficulty starting with the fact that it is a criminal offence to have a cheque referred to drawer for insufficient funds. Equally, casual overdrawing can lead to withdrawal of cheque and banking facilities for a period by the Bank of France. On a positive note, the foregoing means that cheques are readily acceptable and cheque guarantee cards are not yet necessary.

12.2 LOANS FROM A BANK (*CONTRAT DE PRÊT*)

Since there are no special rules relating to the granting of loans in France which differ from practice in the United Kingdom, some points of interest are set out below:

(1) Compound interest

French law does not permit the charging of compound interest (*contrat d'anatocisme*) unless the interest upon which the interest is sought to be charged is owing for a full year. Bank account debit balances, however, may suffer compound interest for periods of less than a year.

(2) Indexation

It is possible in France to index the capital value of a loan by reference to an external measure connected with the purpose of the loan as set out in art 79 of the Ordinance of 30 December 1958. Typically a loan to purchase property might refer to the quarterly Index of Construction Costs (*Indice trimestriel du coût de la construction*) published by INSEE, the national statistics office. Such agreement may not, however, stipulate upwards only movements.

(3) Usurious interest

According to the Law of 28 December 1966 (the '1966 Law' relating to usuary, loans, door-to-door canvassing and advertising requirements) the rate of interest on a loan must be below a maximum rate which is considered to be 'usurious' (*usuaire*). This rate is published by the National Credit Council of the Ministry of the Economy from time to time. Where a loan is granted at a usurious interest rate it is not null and void but any excess interest paid is deducted from future interest or principal payments to be made under the loan. If the principal and interest on the loan have been fully repaid, the lender must reimburse the excess interest paid by the borrower plus interest thereon. In addition, criminal penalties may be imposed on the lender or any person who knowingly assisted in the negotiation or granting of a usurious loan. The foregoing may explain why there are no true credit cards in France.

(4) Effective overall rate (*taux éffectif global*)

The 1966 Law obliges lenders to stipulate an effective overall rate (*taux éffectif global*—TEG) in the loan agreement. Failure to do so invalidates the interest provision of the loan agreement for want of clarity and the legal rate of interest must apply. This is calculated from treasury bond yields and the rate for 1991 was 9.26 per cent. For the purposes of calculating the TEG charged, all commissions, remunerations or other expenses of any nature as well as insurance premiums paid by the borrower for any compulsory insurance must be included.

(5) *Lois Scrivener*

The *Lois Scrivener* of 10 January 1978 and 13 July 1979 provide for consumer credit protection. These laws do not deal with business credit but with credit granted commercially by an individual or a company to consumers.

The 1979 law only concerns real property transactions whilst the 1978 law covers any credit transaction. However, some transactions are excluded from the latter such as credit transactions entered into by means of a notarial deed (*acte authentique*); or for a period equal to or less than three months; or for an amount greater than FF 10,000. Under these laws, the lender has to make a written offer of loan or credit. The acceptance by the borrower of the offer is only final after a 'cooling-off period' of seven days under the 1978 law and ten days under the 1979 law. The offer must state the amount of credit, the conditions for the loan, the insurance to be effected and the TEG. Furthermore, the indemnities stipulated in case of early repayment or termination for breach by the borrower of his obligations are capped. Failure to respect these formalities gives rise to criminal liability.

12.3 LEASING (*Crédit-bail*)

In France leasing is regarded as a financial service whereby a bank or a finance company buys real or personal property at a customer's request and leases it to him at an agreed rental with the option to purchase it at the end of the contract term. The Law of 2 July 1966 applies to:

—leasing transactions involving real property used for professional purposes;
—construction and capital equipment; or
—Goodwill.

If real property is involved, the lease is usually granted by specialist financial companies called SICOMI which benefit from a special tax dispensation enabling them to convey the property at the end of the lease to the lessee at a special stamp duty rate of two per cent.

Leasing must not be confused with hire-purchase (*location-*

vente). In a lease, the lessee is granted rights of enjoyment over the leased property and a unilateral purchase option which he may, but need not, exercise. In a *location-vente* agreement, the lessee is granted rights of enjoyment over the leased property and, in addition, is obliged to purchase the property at the end of the lease. Leasing is also to be distinguished from a lease-back agreement (*lease-back*). In a lease-back agreement, the lessee first sells his property to the lessor who in turn leases it back to him with the possibility of repurchasing it at the end of the lease. Leasing is almost always a three-party transaction whilst in a 'lease-back' the seller of the property is also the future lessee.

In a French *crédit-bail* the lessor grants a power of attorney to the lessee enabling him to decide which supplier will supply the equipment or which real property or Goodwill is to be acquired and then leased to him. The power of attorney is necessary to preserve the lessor's title to the goods acquired and prevent the lessee becoming owner at once. As a result of the power of attorney, the lessor is usually exempted from the warranties normally given to a lessee and the lessee is subrogated to the rights of the lessor against the supplier or vendor. The lessor may also assign to the lessee its rights to bring an action against the supplier or seller for breach of warranty. As a consequence of this power of attorney if the sale agreement is cancelled by the lessee the lease agreement is still binding on him and he has to pay the rent or indemnify the lessor.

Many lease agreements provide that if the lessee breaches the lease obligations bringing the contract to an end, damages equal to the amount of the rent to be paid over the unexpired term of the lease must be paid in damages. The lessee is also obliged to return the leased property and the lessor has to recover it. As a general rule such damage clauses will be applied although the court nevertheless has a discretion to alter the amount of damages in the event that they are manifestly excessive or insufficient.

A lease contains a unilateral purchase option for the lessee. The lease must specify when and under what conditions the option may be exercised. Where the lease relates to real property, the rules and regulations governing unilateral purchase options for real property apply with the exception of the requirement that the unilateral purchase option be registered with the tax authorities. Leases of personal property must be registered on a special register maintained at either the Commercial Court or the Superior Court (*tribunal de grande instance*) for the area in which the lessee does business. Leases of real property of over 12 years must be recorded at the Land Registry. Failure to do so renders the lease void as against third parties.

Equally the lessee must declare, in his financial statements, the yearly rental under any lease and also in a note to the accounts the outstanding payments due under the lease. There are criminal penalties for failure to do so. This limits the possibilities for 'off-balance sheet' lease finance.

12.4 FACTORING

A factoring contract (*contrat d'affacturage*) is a commercial contract whereby a factoring company, known as the factor, agrees to pay to his client which is a seller of goods or services, the claims he has on his own debtors. The factor has to collect his client's debts. The contract may provide for one or more lump sum payments effectively discounting the debts due.

Such an operation constitutes a short-term realisable claims credit (*crédit de mobilisation de créances à court terme*). Once he has advanced the funds, the factor is subrogated to the rights of his client but must give notice of his interest by *huissier*. Alternatively the factor may receive a factoring charge calculated as a percentage of the debts collected. Factoring, although similar to transfer of debts (*cession de créances*) is to be distinguished from it in as much as a factoring agreement usually provides for the grant of an exclusive right by the seller to the factor to collect the seller's debts. The principal advantages of a factoring agreement are the ability of the seller to increase his cash flow by the amount paid for his debts if a lump sum arrangement is made and in either case the separation of the selling and debt collection functions of the seller.

If the seller's invoices contain a clear indication of the fact when they are issued, the purchaser will have proper notice to pay the factor avoiding the need for formal service of any notice by *huissier*.

12.5 CORPORATE FINANCE

12.5.1 DIFFERENT METHODS OF FINANCING A *SOCIÉTÉ ANONYME* (SA)

In addition to the issue of ordinary shares, there are four principal ways in which an SA may obtain finance:

(1) The issue of non-voting preferred stock (*actions à dividende prioritaire sans droit de vote*)

Non-voting preferred stock is issued after the passing of a resolution at an extraordinary general meeting of the shareholders. The SA must have made distributable profits in the two fiscal years preceding such issue and the aggregate amount of the non-voting preferred stock issued must not exceed one-quarter of its registered capital.

(2) Investment and voting certificates (*certificats d'investissements et de droit de vote*)

An SA may, pursuant to a resolution passed at an extraordinary general meeting of the shareholders, break down existing shares or new shares to be issued in connection with an increase in share capital into investment and voting certificates. This is provided, however, that the aggregate value of the SA's investment and voting certificates will not, as a result of the issue, exceed 25 per cent of its registered capital.

(3) Debentures (*Obligations*)

An SA may issue negotiable debentures if the following conditions have been complied with:

—all of its share capital has been paid up,

—it has been in existence for at least two years, and

—it has had its financial statements duly approved by its shareholders for at least two years.

Debentures may be non-convertible, convertible (*obligations convertibles en actions*) or coupled with a stock warrant (*obligation avec bons de souscription d'achat*). In all events, a debenture must have a face value of FF 100 or a multiple thereof.

Where the debentures are non-convertible, their issue must be authorised by the shareholders at an ordinary general meeting. Where the debentures are convertible or coupled with a stock warrant, a resolution must be passed at an extraordinary general meeting of the shareholders. For a public offering a prospectus approved by the COB is prepared and distributed. Once the debentures have been placed, the debenture holders of each particular issue constitute a legal entity (*masse des obligataires*) and benefit from certain rights as a group.

(4) Stock or investment certificate warrants (*Bons de souscription*)

An SA may, if duly authorised by the shareholders at an extraordinary general meeting, issue stock or investment certificate warrants (*bons de souscription*) which entitle the holder thereof to subscribe to shares or investment certificates issued by the SA if:

(i) the extraordinary general meeting has authorised the issue of the shares or investment certificates which are the subject of the stock or investment certificate warrant; and

(ii) the shareholders or holders of investment certificates have waived their pre-emptive right to subscribe to the shares or investment certificates.

(5) Loans

Loans made by shareholders to an SA present a particular problem under French law. The interest paid on such loans is normally deductible by the corporation if the registered capital of the SA is fully paid up.

Such deductions, however, are limited both as to the interest rate charged and the identity of the lending shareholders. The maximum interest rate that will be deductible by the corporation is the annual average effective gross semestrial yield of debentures issued by private corporations during the current calendar year as published by the Ministry of Finance. If the shareholder making a loan actively participates in the management of the company, the interest paid by the company thereon is deductible only to the extent that all loans made to the corporation by the shareholder do not exceed 150 per cent of the registered capital of the SA.

12.5.2 CAPITAL INCREASE

The capital of an SA may be increased either by an issue of new shares or an increase in par value of issued shares. The decision to increase the capital is reserved to the shareholders in an extraordinary general meeting. In the event new shares are to be issued, such issue may not take place before:

(i) the approval, if necessary, of the Treasury Department has been obtained;
(ii) the increase has been recorded in the Register of Commerce and Companies; and
(iii) the payment of all or part of the subscription price and any premium element (*prime d'émission*).

In any event where new shares are to be issued for cash the existing shareholders have a pre-emptive right to receive, *pro rata* to their existing shareholding, any new shares to be issued. Such rights can be varied or suspended in any appropriate case but only by the shareholders themselves in extraordinary general meeting.

12.5.3 LOANS TO OTHER *SOCIÉTÉS*

Members' loans to other forms of *société* (*apports en compte courant*) such as SARL, SNC, *société civile* are possible without undue formality and are very common. The rate of interest paid must be reasonable to be deductible from the profits of the *société*. The amount of loans by the shareholders of a SARL engaged in its management must not exceed 150 per cent of its capital. Equally, the capital of such *sociétés* may be increased at any time consistent with the *statuts* of the *sociétés* concerned. A private placement of debentures is possible for all *sociétés* except an EEIG.

12.6 BANKING OPERATIONS

12.6.1 BANK ACCOUNTS

All business establishments and traders must open a bank account. A company seeking to open such an account will have to produce a certificate attesting to its due registration with the Registry of Commerce and Companies, a copy of its Articles of Incorporation and the authorisation of the representative(s) it has empowered to act on its behalf to deal with the bank. A company in the process of registration (*en formation*) may be permitted to open a bank account if it provides adequate guarantees to the bank. The bank must notify the tax authorities within one month of the closure or modification of the functioning of the bank account.

12.6.2 BANK FACILITIES

Where a bank grants overdraft facilities to a business, the rate of interest which will be charged on the amount of overdraft (*agio*), has to be clearly stipulated in the contract. It is a common practice for banks to grant overdraft facilities on an informal basis for an indefinite period of time. It should be noted that in such case, a bank may, under certain conditions, be held liable for the damages caused to its clients and/or third parties as a result of a sudden and unjustified withdrawal of them.

12.6.3 LIABILITY OF BANKS AND CREDIT ESTABLISHMENTS

Banks may be held liable in tort (*responsabilité délictuelle*) which is governed by art 1382 of the Civil Code or in contract (*responsabilité contractuelle*) which is governed by art 1143 of the Civil Code. Under the former, the plaintiff must prove that:

(i) the bank or other credit establishment committed a wrongful act or omission;
(ii) that he suffered a legally recognisable loss;
(iii) that a causal link exists between such act or omission and his loss.

Thus, a bank or other credit establishment may be liable to third parties in tort if it opens a bank account for a client without first verifying the authenticity and validity of any power of attorney which served to open the account.

Banks and other credit establishments may also be liable in the event that they extend credit to a client who is in an irreversible financial crisis and therefore artificially permit the continuation of his business causing loss to third parties. Similarly, when a bank discounts cheques drawn by a company which it knows to be insolvent or takes other actions which artificially assist its client to defer ceasing to trade (*cessation des paiements*) liability is imposed (see Chapter 11). On the other hand, banks are also subject to liability where they refuse, without just cause or prior notice, to continue an existing oral credit arrangement such as overdraft facilities and as a result of such refusal, its client is forced into bankruptcy.

12.7 Negotiable instruments

12.7.1 BILLS OF EXCHANGE (*Lettres de change ou traites*)

The rules relating to bills of exchange are to be found in the Decree of 30 December 1935. A bill is defined as an order in writing addressed by one person, the drawer (*le tireur*) to another, the drawee (*le tiré*) requiring the person to whom it is addressed to pay, at a fixed time, a sum certain in money to a specified person, the payee (*le bénéficiaire ou preneur*).

To be valid the bill must contain:
(i) the words bill of exchange (*lettre de change*) in French or in the language in which it is drafted;
(ii) an order to pay a sum certain;
(iii) the name and address of the drawee;

(iv) the due date for payment;
(v) the name of the payee;
(vi) the place and date of the issue;
(vii) the place where payment is to take place;
(viii) the signature of the drawer.

If one or more of the above mentioned formalities are not fulfilled, the bill is considered null and void. However there are certain presumptions that may save it. A bill without a date for payment is deemed to be a sight draft. If the address for payment is missing it is deemed payable at the drawee's address on the bill and similarly if the place of issue is missing the bill is deemed issued at the drawer's address. Bills of exchange are stampable with a nominal amount although absence of the stamp will not itself invalidate the bill of exchange. Only sight bills or those payable at a fixed period after presentation may stipulate a specified rate of interest. Any such provision in any other type of bill is void. The rules relating to endorsement, acceptances and *avals* are the same as in English law, although a protest against non-payment by the drawee in France must be delivered by a *huissier* to be effective. The relevant prescription periods are as follows:

(i) three years for an action against the drawee-acceptor;
(ii) one year for an action against the endorser or the drawer if it is brought by the holder;
(iii) six months if it is brought by the endorsee.

Since July 1973, a computer process has been introduced to simplify the collection of the bills of exchange and to reduce costs. This process is known as *lettre de change relevé* (LCR).

12.7.2 CHEQUES

The procedure and practice relating to cheques in France is substantially different from that in England and Wales. As we will see, the formal legal situation and negotiability of cheques are similar.

The rules relating to cheques are to be found in the Decree of 30 December 1935. A cheque is defined as an order addressed by one person to his banker requiring the latter to pay at sight a certain sum of money to the order of a specified person or to bearer.

The cheque is a formal instrument and therefore it must contain the following legal requirements:

    (i)   The word *chèque*;
   (ii)   The date and place of issue;
  (iii)   A mandate to pay a sum certain in money;
  (iv)   The signature of the person who draws the cheque known as the drawer (*tireur*) and name of the person on whom the cheque is drawn known as the drawee (*tiré*);
   (v)   The designation of the person to whom the cheque is payable known as the payee (*bénéficiaire*). It can be to the order of a specified person, to bearer or in blank.

The cheque may be a crossed cheque which means that it may be collected only by a banker. A cheque which has been crossed generally may be crossed by any banker whereas a specially crossed cheque may be collected only by the banker named in the crossing. The cheque may be crossed 'not negotiable' except for a bank. One of the reasons why cheques are not usually negotiable in France is that banks which issue uncrossed cheques to customers must inform the Revenue of the identity of the customer and the numbers of the cheques. The funds to cover the cheque must exist at the date of issue and must be liquid. If the funds in the account are insufficient on presentation, the bank may refuse to pay a cheque issued for an amount superior to FF 100. In this case, if the drawer does not regularise his situation within 30 days following a letter requiring him to do so, sent by his bank, he may have his cheque facilities withdrawn. Indeed, if he has failed in this way within the last twelve months, he does not have the option of covering the cheque and suspension of cheque facilities is automatic as well as notification to the Bank of France.

This sanction may also be applied at any time if the bank has reasonable cause. It is backed by criminal penalties, which, if intent to cause damage is proved, can include a fine of up to FF 2,500,000, imprisonment for up to five years and a ban on issuing cheques for up to five years.

Three fundamental rules govern the delivery of the cheque to the payee (*bénéficiaire*). Firstly, delivery does not involve *novation* of the original debt which means that any security provided for it is unaffected. Secondly, delivery does not constitute payment. Consequently, the place and date of payment will be those of collection (*encaissement*). Thirdly, funds representing the cheque are transferred to the payee at delivery. The rules governing endorsements are similar to those governing bills of exchange (see paragraph **12.7.1**).

As regards payment, a cheque should generally be presented within eight days of its issue. If not, payment is still due by the bank until the expiry of the limitation period which is equal to one year for an action by the holder against the drawee and six months for other actions. Payment is due unless a stop has been put on payment (*opposition*) from the drawer or one of the drawer's creditors. The only two valid reasons for such a stop being put on payment are:

(i) the loss of the cheque
(ii) the bankruptcy of the holder.

Otherwise a stop being put on payment becomes a criminal offence (*délit de blocage de provision*). If the payment is refused, three formalities must be undertaken:

—protest (*protêt*) within the presentation period;
—publication with the clerk of the competent tribunal and notification to the Bank of France (*Banque de France*);
—obtaining a certificate of non-payment which is delivered to the holder and which constitutes sufficient evidence to prove an offence for subsequent criminal procedure.

12.7.3 PROMISSORY NOTES

A promissory note is a promise in writing made by one person known as the drawer (*souscripteur*) undertaking to pay at a fixed time, a sum certain in money, to a specified person known as the payee (*bénéficiaire*). Unlike a bill of exchange, a promissory note involves only two people. As a general rule, the promissory note is subject to the same rules as a bill of exchange but it has some special characteristics. A promissory note is subject to strict

formal requirements and must contain the following matters otherwise it is void:
  (i) the words *billet à ordre*;
  (ii) the date and place of issue;
  (iii) the circumstances of payment (amount, place and date);
  (iv) the obligation to pay;
  (v) the name of the payee; and
  (vi) the drawer's signature.

The drawer of a promissory note differs from the drawer of a bill of exchange in that for a promissory note, there is no underlying third party obligation which is effectively transferred by the instrument (*provision*). Therefore, the holder does not acquire any third party claim, and on the other hand, a holder cannot use the absence of *provision* in order to sue the drawer as may be done on a bill of exchange consideration (*cause*) for the issue of the note is, however, required. Further, the purpose for which a promissory note is used determines its civil or commercial status and therefore the court before which any claim may be pursued.

There is a special form of promissory note called a *warrant* which arises when goods are stored in a public warehouse. This is sufficiently rare to put it outside the scope of this work.

12.7.4 DAILLY'S LAW

Under law No 81-1 of 2 January 1981, known as Dailly's Law, a loan granted by a credit establishment to one of its clients in order to help finance the latter's activities, may be secured by means of transfer or pledge of the client's trade debts. The client to whom such a credit is granted may be either a private or a public legal entity or an individual carrying out a professional or commercial activity. A transfer or pledge of trade debts is recorded by an agreement known as *bordereau de créances professionnelles* which contains certain mandatory provisions.

Any security guaranteeing the debt is transferred with it.

Once the credit establishment has given notice of the execution of the agreement by *huissier* to the debtor of its borrower, such debtor(s) may only satisfy their debts to the borrower by making payment to the credit establishment. If the debtor accepts in writing the transfer of the trade debts, the credit establishment will have the same rights as a holder of an accepted bill of exchange.

12.8 GUARANTEES

12.8.1 CAUTION

Cautionnement is a unilateral contract whereby the guarantor (*caution*) undertakes to a creditor to execute the debtor's obligations in the event that the latter fails to execute them. Such guarantee may be given for a definite or indefinite sum. In the event that a specific limitation on the guarantee is made, according to art 1326 of the Civil Code, the sum must be written in letters and figures. In this case the guarantor is not liable beyond such sum except if he has expressly agreed also to guarantee interest and costs. However, if the guarantor has not specified the exact debt to be guaranteed, the guarantee covers not only the underlying debt but all incidental costs, charges and expenses relating thereto. Where a guarantee is given for an indefinite sum, the Supreme Court has stated that the guarantor must have expressly written that he has knowledge of the nature and the extent of his obligation. In order to protect the guarantor, the Supreme Court has held guarantees null and void where this requirement has not been fulfilled. Where the guarantor is called upon to perform under a guarantee, he has the right to require the creditor to first proceed against the property of the principal debtor unless he has specifically waived such right. This right is known as the *bénéfice de discussion*.

Where there are several guarantors of the same debt, each one of them is, as a general rule, deemed to guarantee the entire debt. Nevertheless, each guarantor has the right to require the creditor to commence a separate action against him for his *pro rata* share of the principal debt (*bénéfice de division*) unless he has specifically waived such right. Where, however, the guarantor has agreed to be jointly and severally liable with other guarantors and the debtor (*cautionnement solidaire*), he does not benefit from these rights. If the principal debtor fails, such guarantor may be sued by the creditor for the entire amount of the debt even if an action has not been brought against the debtor and the other guarantors.

Where the guarantor has performed under the guarantee, he is subrogated to all of the rights of the creditor against the debtor.

Unlike in England, the guarantor may defend an action on a guarantee upon the basis that the underlying contract is inchoate or otherwise void. For this reason another type of guarantee known as a First Demand Guarantee can be given.

12.8.2 FIRST DEMAND GUARANTEE (*Garantie à première demande*)

The French system has adopted a guarantee similar to a first demand guarantee in England (*garantie à première demande*).

Unlike the general rule in guarantees mentioned above, the recent jurisprudence from the Supreme Court has decided that a first demand guarantor may not raise defences based on the nullity of the principal agreement nor the incorrect execution nor any other matter which the principal obligor might raise.

Such guarantees contain the words 'first demand' and typically renounce the *bénéfice de discussion* or *de division* referred to above. They are now the more common form of bank guarantee in international contracts.

12.8.3 GUARANTEES BY SAs

A special word needs to be said about the giving of corporate guarantees, by a French SA art. 98 of the Law of 24 July 1966 (66–537) ('The 1966 law') together with art. 89 of the Decree of 31 December 1967 (67–1255) prescribes a number of requirements which are considered to be matters of public order (*ordre public*) and therefore may not be excluded. Taken together they make the accepting of a guarantee by an SA a matter to which special care needs to be applied and constitute an exception to the rule that board resolutions are not required to support the authority of the PDG.

Briefly, an SA may not grant a guarantee of third party obligations, including those of a subsidiary, unless the board by resolution have authorised the PDG so to do. Article 117 of the 1966 Law gives the Director General (*directeur général*) the same powers as the PDG and in any event the PDG may delegate the authority given to him by the board by way of specific power of attorney (*pouvoir*). The authority given to the PDG must be renewed at least annually. The resolution must authorise either the specific transaction or an overall maximum together with a maximum individual limit for any one guarantee to be given under the general authority. The beneficiary of the guarantee has a positive obligation of due diligence to require sight of the resolution and satisfy itself that the guarantee is validly authorised (JCP 1989 II 21305). If it fails to do so the guarantee is unenforceable. The beneficiary will be protected, however, if the overall maximum has, in fact, been exceeded provided that the guarantee in question does not itself exceed either the overall maximum or the specified individual maximum and it was unaware of the exceeding of the limit. This obligation of due diligence extends equally to foreign corporations. (Cass. Comm 29 July 1980 Bull IV.36)

Accordingly, the giving of an unlimited guarantee by an SA is highly problematical. The only truly safe course is to require the guarantor to enter into the contract giving rise to the obligation guaranteed either initially or by way of subsequent novation. If the SA guarantor is thus made a primary obligor the formal requirements mentioned are not relevant. They do not apply, in any event, to a bank or credit establishment granting guarantees in the ordinary course of business. Unlimited guarantees may, nonetheless be given in favour of the tax and customs authorities.

13
ENVIRONMENT AND PLANNING

13.1 ENVIRONMENTAL PROTECTION

France has taken various measures designed to protect the environment both of its own motion and as a result of the European initiatives in this area which are contained in the various EEC directives.

This chapter attempts to deal with those environmental matters which are likely to impact on commercial ventures of a general nature. Environmental issues arising from maritime and ultra-hazardous operations are considered to be outside the scope of this work. Suffice to say that these matters are the subject of laws of both civil and criminal nature. Maritime legislation has been considerably strengthened in the wake of disasters such as the *Amoco Cadiz* and the *Tanio* which had serious effects on the coastal waters of Brittany and Normandy.

Environmental protection issues for the purposes of this work fall into two main categories:

(1) Planning control matters relating to new projects which are likely to have a negative environmental impact such as the building or extension of industrial processing plants or the creation of mineral extraction facilities both on and off-shore.

(2) Matters relating to the control of emissions and disposal of waste products including domestic waste (*ordures ménagères*) and agricultural chemicals.

13.1.1 PLANNING CONTROLS

Planning control issues are dealt with under French planning legislation and are subject to the control of the local planning authorities, usually the mayor (*maire*) of the *commune* in which the particular installation or facility is sought to be developed. The authorities have a general mandate, if they have adopted a land use plan (*plan de l'occupation du sol* or POS), and the vast majority have done so, to determine priorities and zone particular areas for industrial activities taking into consideration possible polluting effects including not only pollution emissions but also noise. Accordingly, any new building or development works will generally be within the purview of the *maire* of the *commune* in question.

However, France has a system of controls over, *inter alia*, new industrial installations quite independent of planning procedures as such, which is within the jurisdiction of the state governor (*commissaire de la république*) of the district (*département*) in which the proposed development will occur. Such developments are known as classified installations (*installations classées*).

(1) *Installations classées*

These fall into two categories:
- (i) those requiring prior authorisation (*autorisation préalable*) which include most industrial plants, slaughter houses, intensive farming units, boiler plants, infill sites and the like.
- (ii) those requiring a declaration procedure (*déclaration*) which are essentially agricultural installations, vehicle repair shops, small artisanal dyeing and textile plants, etc.

The *Journal Officiel* publishes each year a list (*nomenclature*) of all classified installations, each one preceded by an A or a D depending upon the procedure applicable. There are currently about 50,000 A installations and about 450,000 D ones.

- (i) Application for *autorisation* is made to the *commissaire* with very full details of the proposal. This triggers:

  —a public enquiry at the expense of the applicant which will last at least a month.

  —consultation procedures with the local council (*conseil municipal*) concerned for which there are strict time limits.

  Once authorised, a copy of the authorisation (*arrêté préfectoral d'autorisation*) must be filed at the local *mairie* and an extract displayed for the general public.

(ii) *Déclarations* are also made to the *commissaire*, although less detail is required. He may accept the *déclaration* as it is, having previously canvassed the views of the local *maire* or impose conditions designed to limit any public nuisance. The *maire* must post in the *mairie* details of the *déclaration* together with any applicable general conditions relating to the activity in question.

The local council or other interested parties may appeal from an *autorisation* or the acceptance of a *déclaration* to the local Administrative Court (*cour administratif*). This must be done within four years of the publication of the decision and the court has wide powers to quash the contested decision, to modify it, to impose additional conditions and even to award damages for abuse of executive powers by the *commissaire*.

In any event, any proposal for a development which requires an *autorisation* must be accompanied by an environmental impact survey (*étude d'impact*).

(2) Etude d'impact

(i) The basic rule is that these are required for all developments, whether they are carried out by public or private entities, unless specifically exempted. There are many such exemptions. However, a survey is always required for:
—mining operations;
—underground hydrocarbon and chemical storage;
—*installations classées* requiring *autorisation*;
—nuclear power stations;
—certain large scale agricultural activities;
—high voltage power lines over 225 KV;
—hydroelectric dams producing more than 500 KW;

—caravan sites for more than 200;
—sewage and waste treatment plants for towns of more than 10,000 inhabitants.

These are produced at the applicant's expense.

(ii) They must contain four elements:
—a study of the present state of the site and its environs, including neighbouring land use and occupation;
—an analysis of the effect of the proposed development on the natural habitat, fauna and flora, biological balance, and amenity in the broadest sense;
—the environmental justification(s) for undertaking the development with particular reference to the methods chosen; and
—the measures proposed to avoid, limit or compensate for any negative environmental effects together with an estimate of their related costs.

The latter may refer to any anti-noise barriers or effluent treatments as well as proposals for landscaping or the provision, at the applicant's expense, of alternative habitats for displaced wildlife.

If the development is one necessitating a public enquiry, the *étude d'impact* will be published at the enquiry itself. If no enquiry is required, it will be published with the relevant decisions.

The contents of the *étude d'impact* are studied by the various interested governmental bodies at *département* and *région* level in conjunction with the local *préfecture*. The departments most likely to be involved are:
—forestry and agriculture
—maritime
—industry and research
—architecture and environment

The *commissaire* or any interested service may comment on the *étude d'impact* and raise requisitions seeking further and better particulars.

The Environment Ministry may call for an *étude d'impact* either of its own motion or at the request of any interested person.

13.1.2 WASTE AND EMISSION CONTROL

French law governing industrial waste and emission control is divided into three areas:
(1) solid waste and non-aequous liquids;
(2) contaminated water;
(3) emissions of gas-phase pollutants into the air.

There are separate statutes that apply to each, although for new installations, particularly those requiring *autorisations préalables*, all these matters will be dealt with in some detail at the planning control level and any relevant action stipulated at that time.

For the first two types of waste, the basic principle is that the *commune* in which the installation is situated is obliged to deal with the treatment and disposal of such waste. However, the *Code de l'Urbanisme* dispenses the local authorities from its obligations in that respect if the waste is too unusual or too toxic to be dealt with in the normal way. In such a case the site owner or occupier is obliged to deal with the waste under the supervision of the local authorities represented by the *maire*.

If he does not he may be prosecuted and in appropriate circumstances an administrative charge may be placed on the property (*servitude administrative*).

Compliance is policed by the *maire* under art L131–2 of the *Code des Communes* and by application of arts L160–1 and L480 *et seq* of the *Code de l'Urbanisme* which imposes fines of up to FF 500,000 for violation of planning restrictions including those relating to pollution. For a second offence of the same nature a prison sentence of up to six months may be ordered. Stop orders and daily fines may also be imposed.

In practice it is the civil police (*police judiciaire*) who attends on the offending premises to determine the facts and their preliminary finding (*procès-verbal d'infraction*) is final until the contrary is proved. Enforcement proceedings are brought in the appropriate court and will involve the PDG of an SA or *gérant* of any other *société* as well as any manager actually responsible. A civil action may be brought by an environmental association which, in common with the *maire*, may claim damages on behalf of the community as a *partie civile*.

Water pollution is also sanctioned if wildlife, especially fish, are affected. Article 402 of the *Code Rural* imposes fines up to FF 120,000 for this offence and/or a prison sentence of up to two years. There are similar dispositions if toxic waste affects other animal habitats.

Air pollution standards are imposed on industrial installations at the planning stage and are sanctioned in the same way if they are not observed. Car exhaust emissions are policed under the *Code de la Route* by the *police judiciaire*.

The factories inspectorate (*inspecteurs des installations classées*) is informed of any offence of an environmental nature by the *maire* of any such installation.

Pollution of the environment may, in any event, give rise to civil liability on the basis of art 1382 of the Civil Code at the suit of any party who has suffered loss, including the local *commune* or, in exceptional cases, such as the *Amoco Cadiz*, by the State. In addition and on the same basis damages can be claimed in any criminal action by an injured party who becomes a *partie civile* to the action. A decision finding the defendant guilty will generally found the civil liability claim, although quantum must be established in the usual way.

There are specific statutory provisions relating to pollution arising from agricultural processes such as fertilizers and the use of slurries which are beyond the scope of this section.

13.1.3 EEC DIRECTIVES

As mentioned previously, France has fully implemented these in its domestic laws, following a *Conseil d'Etat* decision of October 1989 in the '*Nicolo*' case. In particular the fourth

Directive on Environmental Audits will impose considerable extra burdens requiring as it does periodic surveys similar to the *étude d'impact* mentioned in section **13.1.1**. Legislation is being introduced to bring this into effect shortly.

13.2 PLANNING

In common with England and Wales the use of land in France is closely controlled, and so changes of use require consent from the competent local authority. This is the mayor (*maire*) of the town or *commune*, in which the property is situated, who delivers a planning consent (*permis de construire*). Permission is also generally required to demolish buildings (*permis de démolir*). An architect (*architecte*) must be involved in any planning application and must sign the proposal. There is no French equivalent of the profession of surveyor, although some English firms are established in Paris and other provincial centres who can perform this service. Civil Engineers (*ingénieurs de génie civile*) are available to advise on technical matters.

The uses to which land is put are generally categorised as:

(i) residential (*logement*)
(ii) commercial (*commercial*)
(iii) professional (*professionnel*)
(iv) agriculture (*agriculture*)
(v) forestry (*forestier*).

Commercial use covers offices as well as other commercial and industrial uses. Control over changes within a designated use class are in general less vigorous than in England, for example shop premises can be used as offices.

There are, however, special requirements for certain types of commerce such as restaurants and take-away food shops. Professional user is not really a separate use class but rather a subclass of residential. In France, in certain circumstances, residential property may be used as offices or consulting rooms by members of one of the liberal professions such as doctors, lawyers, architects and the like. Since 1986 the permission for such exceptional use (*dérogation*) is personal to the professional and does not attach to the property itself, so that once the professional occupancy ceases consent will be required for a new one. This problem can be alleviated by forming an SCP (*société civile professionnelle*) which is similar to an English partnership although it has a legal personality, or an SCM (*société civile de moyens*), a cost sharing vehicle which does not generate profits and is otherwise similar to an SCP. Since both these corporations have legal personalities separate from their members, if they occupy the premises, members may retire without disturbing the use position. Indeed, it is not uncommon for leased premises to be disposed of by all members of an SCM retiring *en bloc* and new members taking their place, so neatly avoiding the need for both a licence to assign the lease and a new *dérogation*. Since 1986, a professional may only occupy 40 square metres of residential space for professional purposes. Thus, four principals may occupy 160 square metres and so forth. A *dérogation* can be obtained by the owner or lessor of residential premises for more than 40 square metres per principal but only if equivalent commercial space in the same ownership in the same *commune* becomes residential. In practice, this is seldom economically viable except in the case of high value rental premises in (say) central Paris and commercial premises in a less favoured *arrondissement*.

It is generally possible to obtain permission for a change of use from (say) residential to commercial by paying a premium to the *commune*. However, such changes are discretionary and may involve compensating changes in the other direction. In Paris and other large cities there is a marked unwillingness to further deplete residential housing stock in established business areas, not least one supposes because it further reduces the number of potential voters.

France has a highly centralised formalistic approach to land use generally and on a grand scale. Each administrative region must have a land use plan (*plan de l'occupation du sol*). This is known as the POS and specifies the existing uses of land zoning areas for particular use and designating areas for special assistance such as special development zones (*zones d'aménagement concertées*) and the like. The POS will tell you most of the information you need about any potential development and in particular whether it fits into the scheme of things envisaged by it. The POS will also deal with proportions of commercial to residential use, percentage of office use within commercial and similar matters. French planning law also uses the notion of the land occupation coefficient (*coefficient de l'occupation du sol*) known as the COS. This defines the maximum permitted construction density for any given site. Paris raised this to 3:1 recently. Thus a site of 100 square metres may, as of right, have 300 square metres of building erected upon it. Subterranean space does not generally count nor do parking spaces. The COS fixes the legal maximum density (*plafond légal de densité*) or PLD. The *commune* may authorise construction in excess of the PLD upon application but the site owner must pay a premium (*réfaction* or *indemnité de dépassement*). This is determined by the Inland Revenue, *fisc*, upon the basis of the value of the undeveloped land required to authorise the excess. There is an appeal from this assessment. The indemnity thus determined is payable in two equal parts, the first 18 months after the date of the application and the second months thereafter.

As can be seen, planning law in France is hedged about with legal constraints and formal legal requirements and all this section can do is give a flavour of what is involved. Once again timely legal advice is crucial to the establishment of a viable project, and any assumption that the matter will proceed upon similar lines to English practice is probably incorrect.

LEGISLATION TABLE

	Page

English Legislation

Fair Trading Act 1973 72

Sale of Goods Act 1979 1

Competition Act 1980 71

Copyright Designs and Patents Act 1988 13

    ss 79–83 17

Companies Act 1989 48

French Legislation
Codes

Civil Code (Code Civil) 1, 63, 66, 82, 95

    art 517 109

    art 1134 2

    art 1143 173

    art 1166 96

    art 1244 163

    art 1326 179

    art 1382 .... 1, 38, 43, 107, 173, 186

    art 1832–1844 49

    art 1984 89

    art 1985 94

    art 2279 160

Code (Code des Communes)—

    art L131–2 185

Code (Code de la Route) 186

Rural Code (Code Rural)—

    art 402 186

Code (Code de l'Urbanisme) 185

    arts L160–1, L480 185

Commercial Code (Code de Commerce) 1, 63, 82, 97

    art 74 97

    art 94 95

Commercial Code (Code de Commerce)—contd
  art 109 2
  art 632 95
Employment Code (Code du Travail) 1, 125, 133
  art L143, 11, 1 159
Penal Code (Code Pénal)—
  arts 177, 179 21
  art 418 20
  art 425(3) 18
Tax Code (Code Général des Impôts) 1
  arts 206, 1 68
  art 257 112
  art 209A 143
Tax Procedure Code (Livre de Procedure Fiscale)— 145
  art L64 82

Decrees

30 October 1935 .... 174, 175
30 September 1953 (No 53–900) 116, 117
23 December 1958 (No 58–1345) 89, 90, 99
  art 1 89
  art 3 94
23 March 1967 (No 67–236) 71
23 March 1967 (No 67–327) 47, 48
23 September 1967 (No 67–821) 49
22 August 1968 (No 68–765) 89, 90
14 March 1986 (No 86–465) 81
22 April 1988 (No 88–418) 71

Regulations

28 September 1989 COB Rules 87

Laws

14 July 1909—
  art 2 22
10 March 1956 (No 56–277) 81
11 March 1957 (No 57–298) 16, 24, 26
  art 6(1) 17

Laws—*contd*
11 March (1957)—*contd*
  art 30(2) 23
  arts 35, 37 18
8 July 1964 (No 64–689) 19
2 July 1966 (No 66–455) 167
24 July 1966 (No 66–537) 48, 54
  art 101 55
  arts L371–389 71
26 December 1966 (No 66–962)—
  art 5 25
28 December 1966 (No 66–1010) 166
13 July 1967 (No 67–563) 147–49, 15
13 July 1979 .... 166, 167
12 May 1980 (No 80–335) 160
2 January 1981 (No 81–1) 178
30 April 1983 (No 85–353) 49
1 March 1984 (No 84–148) 147–52, 155, 157–59, 163
3 January 1985 (No 85–11) 49
25 January 1985 (No 85–88/85–89) 147–49, 151, 152, 155, 157–59, 163
  art 40 .... 157, 159
3 July 1985 (No 85–660) 17
7 July 1985 (No 85–69) 57
25 July 1985 (No 85–772)—
  art 121.2 160
  art 182 161
5 January 1988 (No 88–17) 71, 73
2 August 1989 (No 89–531) 85
13 June 1989 (No 89–377) 60
31 December 1989 (No 89–1010) 162

Ordinances
30 December 1958 (No 58–1374)—
  art 79 165
23 September 1967 (No 67–821) 59
28 September 1967 (No 67—833) 49
1 December 1986 (No 86–1243) 40, 42, 87, 99, 100

Ordinances—contd
1 December 1986—contd
- arts 7–10 .... 40, 41
- art 10(1) 100
- art 36(1), (2) 100

Cases

Cass civ comm 51966 Bull Civ III 351 44
Cass civ comm (1973) DS Jur 587 44
Cass civ comm 29 October 1979 90
Cass civ comm 28 October 1980 90
Cass civ comm (1980) Bull Civ IV 130 46
Cass civ comm (1980) Bull Civ IV 198 45
Cass civ comm (1985) Bull Civ IV 143 105
Cass civ comm 4 November 1986 155
Cass civ comm (1986) DS Jur 436 44
Cass crim (1973) DS Jur 677 101
Cass crim (1983) DS Jur som 211 105
Conseil d'Etat Decision of October 1989 in 'Nicolo' case 186
Cour d'Appel Paris (1977) DS Jur IR 332 45
JCPI (1965) No 76218 102
Rev Tri Dr Com 593 (1978) 103
TGI Bressuire (1974) DSJ 105 107
Trib Corr Paris (1974) BFFF 209 107

European Legislation

European Court Decision of 28 January 1986 (CJCE 28/1/86:
    Cour de Justice de la Cour Européenne'; RTDE 86 p28: 'Revue
    Trimestrielle de Droit Européene 108
EC Directive on Environmental Audits 187
EC Notice on Agreements of Minor Importance OJ (1986) C231/2 30
EC Regulation 1983/83 .... 32, 33
        1984/83 .... 32, 33
        2349/84 .... 25, 33, 36
        123/85 33
        417/85 .... 34, 36
        418/85 .... 33, 36

European Legislation—*contd*
EC Regulation—*contd*
    2137/85 60
    4087/88 .... 35, 36
    559/89 .... 35, 36
LOCE NoC 229/3 of 1987 106
Treaty of Rome 125
  art 85 .... 28, 29, 38, 40, 42
    (1) 28–31, 37, 38, 108
    (2) 37, 41
    (3) 31, 32, 36, 37, 39
  art 86 .... 28, 38–42

International Legislation
Madrid Agreement 16
Bern Convention for the Protection of Literary and Artistic Works 1974 ... 19
Economic Community Patent Convention 1975 12
Geneva Convention on Copyright Protection 12
Geneva Convention Universal Copyright 1952 19
Munich Convention 1973 12
Paris Convention for the Protection of Industrial Property 12, 15, 23
Patent Co-operation Treaty 1970 12

INDEX

Access to information—
  shareholders' rights, 61
Accounts—
  bank, 50
  taxation, 137, 173
Acquisition—
  bloc de contrôle, of, 86
  goodwill, of, 77–81
  public company, of,
    anti-trust provisions, 87–88
    bloc de contrôle, acquisition of, 86
    COB, 85–86
    generally, 85
    take-over bid, 86–87
  shares, 82–85
Advertising—
  misleading, 42–43
  unfair, 44
Agency—
  background, 89
  broker, 97
  commercial agent,
    agreement appointing, 90
    meaning, 89–90
  commission agent,
    agreement, 95–96
    purchase, 95
    sales, 95
    unjust enrichment, action for, 96–97
  independent agent, 94–95

Agency—*contd*
  performance of contract,
    agent, duties of, 90–92
    principal, duties of, 92–93
  sales representative, 98
  termination of contract,
    for cause, 93
    without cause, 93–94
Agent commercial, *See* Commercial agent
Agent d'affaire, *See* Independent agent
Agreement—
  commercial agent, appointment of, 90
  distributorship, *See* Distributorship agreement
  franchise, *See* Franchise agreement
  prohibition of, 29
Amber light proceedings—
  insolvency, measures intended to prevent, 150
Anti-trust provisions—
  public company, acquisition of, 87–88
Appeal—
  Conseil d'Etat, to, 4
  court of appeal, to, 4
  preliminary court, from, 4
  Supreme Court, to, 4

Index

Articles of association—
  preparation of, 49–50
Avocat—
  conseil juridique, fusion of profession with, 5
  new profession of, 5

Banks—
  accounts, 50, 173
  cheques, 175–177
  facilities, 173
  liability of, 173–174
  loans from, 165–167
Bills of exchange—
  rules relating to, 174–175
Bloc de contrôle—
  acquisition of, 86
Board of directors—
  société anonyme, 54–55
Body corporate, *See* Corporate body
Branches—
  business organisation, 69–70
Brevet. *See* Patents
Broker—
  commission, 97
  due diligence, obligation of, 97
  duties of, 97
  good faith, obligation of, 97
Bulletin Officiel de la Propriété Industrielle (BOPI)—
  grant of patents published in, 13
Business—
  insolvency, 148–150
  insolvent, management of, 160–162
  lease, *See* Lease
  organisation, *See* Business organisation

Business—*contd*
  taxation—
    corporate profit, meaning, 142–143
    direct, 138–139
    indirect, 141–142
    tax incentives, 139–141
Business Formalities Centre—
  société, incorporation of, 51–52
Business organisation—
  branches, 69–70
  corporate body, *See* Corporate body
  corporation tax, 68
  generally, 47–48
  liability—
    company, of, 62–63
    directors, of, 63
    managers, of, 63
    members, of, 62
  limited liability company, *See* Limited liability company
  partnership, *See* Partnership
  personal income tax, 68
  registration tax, 68–69
  shareholders, *See* Shareholders
  sole trader, *See* Sole trader
  taxation—
    corporation tax, 68
    personal income tax, 68
    registration tax, 68–69

COB, *See* Stock Exchange Commission
Capital—
  SARL, of, 58
  société anonyme, of, 53–54

Chairman—
  société anonyme, 55
Cheques—
  practice and procedure relating to, 175–177
Chief Executive—
  société anonyme, 55
Civil company—
  activities of, 65–66
  decisions of members, 66
  form of, 66
Commerçant, *See* Sole trader
Commercial agent—
  agreement by which appointed, 90
  meaning, 89–90
Commercial Court—
  commercial disputes between commercial people heard before, 3
  lay judge, 3
  project must be filed with, 73
  status to appear in, 3–4
Commission agent—
  agreement, 95–96
  purchase, 95
  sales, 95
  unjust enrichment, action for, 96–97
Commissionnaire, *See* Commission agent
Committee—
  worker representation, 133
Companies Registry—
  incorporation, filing of documents on, 50–51
Company, *See* Corporate body

Competition—
  block exemption—
    exclusive distribution agreement, 32
    exclusive purchasing agreement, 32–33
    franchise agreement, 35
    generally, 32
    know-how licensing agreement, 35
    motor vehicle, exclusive distribution of, 33
    patent licensing agreement, 33
    research and development agreement, 34–35
    specialisation agreement, 34
  distortion of, 30
  dominant position—
    abuse of, 39
    relevant market, 38
    when existing, 39
  EEC law—
    Article 86, 38–39
    block exemptions, 32–35
    exemptions, 31–32
    generally, 28
    individual exemptions, 36
    notification to Commission, 36–37
    opposition procedure, 36
    prohibition, 28–31
    violation, consequences of, 37–38
Exemptions,
  block, 32–35
  generally, 31–32
  individual, 36

Index

Competition—*contd*
  French law,
    articles 7–10, 40–41
    Competition Council, 42
    enticing personnel, 45
    generally, 39–40
    misleading advertising, 42–43
    passing off, 44
    relief, 46
    slander of goods, 45
    trade libel, 45
    trade secrets, misuse of, 45
    transparency, 42–43
    unfair advertising, 44
    unfair competition, 43–44
  notification to Commission, 36–37
  opposition procedure, 36
  prevention of, 30
  prohibited behaviour, examples of, 31
  restriction of, 30
  unfair, *See* Unfair competition
Competition Council—
  powers of, 42
Completion—
  sale and purchase, 112
Concentration, *See* Dominant position
Concerted practices—
  prohibition of, 29
Confidential information—
  procedure, 19
Conseil d'Etat—
  appeal to, 4
Conseil juridique—
  avocat, fusion of profession with, 5

Conseil juridique—*contd*
  commercial contract, drafting of, 8
  court, may not appear in, 8
Contract—
  agency, termination of—
    for cause, 93
    without cause, 93–94
  employment, *See* Employment
  performance of—
    agent, duties of, 90–92
    principal, duties of, 92–93
  sale of land, 110–111
  supply, 104
Copyright—
  artistic creation, rights attaching to, 17
  exploitation, 17–19
  financial nature, rights deriving from work of, 17
  generally, 16
  painter, rights of, 16
  procedure, 16–17
  protection, 17–19
  remedies, 17–19
  sculptor, rights of, 16
  works entitled to protection, 16–17
Corporate body—
  basis of, 48
  categories of, 47
  commercial and civil distinguished, 47–48
  finance, *See* Financing company
  incorporation—
    articles of association, preparation of, 49–50
    bank account, opening of, 50

Corporate body—*contd*
  incorporation—*contd*
    business formalities centre, 51–52
    Companies Registry, 50–51
    generally, 49
    publishing notice, 50
    registration tax, payment of, 50
    shareholders, execution of statuts by, 50
  legal personality, 47
  legislation, 48–49
  liability of, 62–63
  limited liability company, *See* Limited liability company
  private company, *See* Private company
  public company, *See* Public company
  ultra vires, doctrine of, 48
Corporate profit—
  meaning, 142–143
Corporation tax—
  rate of, 68
Court bailiff—
  function of, 9
  originating process served by, 4
  patents, protection of, 13
Court of appeal—
  preliminary court, appeal from, 4
Courtier, *See* Broker
Courts—
  administrative function, 8–9
  inquisitorial nature of, 4
  three levels of jurisdiction, 3
Credit establishments—
  liability of, 173–174

Credit-bail, *See* Leasing
Creditors—
  insolvency, rights relating to, 159–160

Débauchage, *See* Personnel
Decisions—
  prohibition of, 29
Design—
  procedure for registration, 22–23
  protection, 23–24
  registered, 21–22
  transfer, 23–24
  use, 23–24
Development, *See* Research and development
Directors—
  liability of, 63
  société anonyme, 56
Disciplinary sanctions—
  employment contract, 129
Dismissal—
  collective, 130–131
  employment contract, 130–132
  unfair, 131
Distribution—
  motor vehicle, of, block exemption relating to, 33
Distributorship agreement—
  approved, 105
  exclusive—
    block exemption, 32
    distributor, obligations imposed on, 102–103
    duration of exclusivity, 101
    grantor, obligations imposed on, 102

Distributorship agreement—*contd*
  exclusive—*contd*
    obligations imposed by,
      101–104
    price-fixing, 101
    refusal to deal, 100–101
    restraint of trade, 101
    termination of, 103–104
    validity of, 99–101
  nature of, 99
  non-exclusive, 104–105
  selective, 104–105
  supply contract, 104
  types of, 99
Dominant position—
  abuse of, 39
  anti-trust provisions, 87–88
  article 86, prohibition of, 39
  relevant market, 38

Economic Interest Group—
  Europe, 60
  France, 59–60
Emissions—
  control of, 185–186
Employee—
  profit sharing scheme, 134
  right to work, 123–124
Employment—
  contract—
    collective dismissal, 130–131
    dismissal, 130–132
    fixed term, 126
    indefinite term, 126
    internal regulations, 128
    salary, 127
    suspension, 128

Employment—*contd*
  contract—*contd*
    temporary staff, 126–127
    termination, 128–130
    third party, obligations to, 127
    trial period, 127
    unfair dismissal, 131–132
    variation, 128
  employee profit sharing scheme,
    134
  legislation, 125–126
  maternity leave, 135–136
  share options, 135
  social security system, 135
  worker representation—
    committee, 133
    staff representatives, 133
    trade union, 133
  working conditions, 132–133
English law—
  French law distinguished from,
    1–3
Entreprise individuelle, *See* Sole
  trader
Environmental protection—
  categories of, 181
  EEC Directive, 186–187
  emission control, 185–186
  planning, 181–185
  waste control, 185–189
European Economic Community—
  competition law—
    article 86, 38–39
    block exemptions, 32–35
    exemptions, 31–32
    generally, 28
    individual exemptions, 36

European Economic
Community—*contd*
competition law—*contd*
notification to Commission,
36–37
opposition procedure, 36
prohibition, 28–31
violation, consequences of, 37–38
Economic Interest Group, 60
environmental protection, 186–187
immigration—
EEC nationals, 125
non-EEC nationals, 123–125
treaty of Rome, 28
Exclusive distributorship agreement,
See Distributorship
Exploitation—
copyright, of, 17–19

Factoring—
financing company, 169
Financing company—
banking operations—
accounts, 173
facilities, 173
liability, 173–174
credit establishments, liability of,
173–174
factoring, 169
generally, 165
guarantees—
caution, 179–180
first demand, 180
leasing, 167–169
loans—
bank, from, 165–167
société anonyme, for, 171–172

Financing company—*contd*
negotiable instruments—
bills of exchange, 174–175
cheques, 175–177
Dailly's law, 178
promissory notes, 177–178
société anonyme—
capital increase, 172
debentures, 170–171
investment, 170
loans, 171–173
non-voting preferred stock, 170
stock or investment certificate
warrant, 171
voting certificates, 170
Fonds de commerce, See Goodwill
Franchise agreement—
background, 106
block exemption relating to, 35
exclusivity—
franchise, 108
pronuptia litigation, 108
termination, 108
franchisee's activities, control of,
107
industrial property, franchise as
licence of, 107
intellectual property, franchise as
licence of, 107
know-how transfer, franchise as, 107
termination, 108
French law—
English law distinguished from,
1–3
Fusion, See Merger
General partnership—
nature of, 64

Index

Germany—
  legal advice, monopoly over supplying, 5
Goods—
  slander of, 45
Goodwill—
  acquisition of, 77–81
  agreement to purchase, 78–79
  asset acquisition, 78
  business lease, 117–119
  lease of, 81–82
  sale of, 80–81
  sole trader, of, 67–68
  transfers of, 81
  vendor—
    lien on goodwill, 80
    warranties given by, 79–80
Grantor—
  exclusive distributorship agreement, obligations relating to, 102
Guarantees—
  caution, 179–180
  first demand, 180

Hive-off—
  expert, appointment of, 73–74
  nature of, 71
  provisions governing, 71
  shareholders, meeting of, 74
  tax treatment, 75–77
  terms and conditions, 72–73
Huissier, *See* Court bailiff

INPI, *See* Institut National de la Propriété Industrielle
Imitation, *See* Passing-off

Immigration—
  EEC nationals, 125
  non-EEC nationals, professional, 125
  right to reside, 123
  right to work, 123–124
  self-employed, 124–125
Income tax—
  direct personal tax, as, 143–145
  personal, 68
Incorporation, *See* Corporate body
Independent agent—
  agreement with, 94
  commission, 94
  principal, contract with, 94
  termination of authority, 94–95
Industrial property—
  franchise as licence of, 107
  intellectual property distinguished from, 12
  patents, *See* Patents
Inferior court—
  non-commercial cases heard by, 4
Information—
  access to, shareholders' rights, 61
  confidential, 19
Insolvency—
  business, 148–150
  creditors, rights of, 159–160
  generally, 147–148
  management, responsibilities and liabilities of, 160–162
  measures intended to prevent—
    amber light proceedings, 150
    initiation of proceedings, 151–152
    moratoria, 150–151

Insolvency—*contd*
  measures intended to prevent—*contd*
    rehabilitation proceedings, 152–159
    winding-up, 151
  personal, 162–164
  practitioner, 153–154
  rehabilitation proceedings—
    different steps in, 154–159
    participants in, 152–154
Institut National de la Propriété Industrielle (INPI)—
  patent applications dealt with by, 13
  trademarks, procedure relating to, 14–15
Intellectual property—
  copyright, *See* Copyright
  franchise as licence of, 107
  industrial property distinguished from, 12
Investigation—
  taxation, 137
Investment—
  restrictions on, 31

Judges—
  appeal, 4

Know-how
  franchise as transfer, 107
  licensing—
    agreement, block exemption relating to, 35
    form, 25–27
    generally, 25

Know-how—*contd*
  licensing—*contd*
    procedure, 25–27
  meaning, 20
  moral element, lack of, 21
  procedure, 19–21
  protection, 21
  transfer, 21, 107

Land, *See* Real property
Lawyers—
  activities incompatible with practice of law, 6–9
  administration of law by, 5–6
  monopoly, lack of, 5
Lease—
  business—
    conditions to be satisfied, 116
    goodwill, 117–119
    possession after three-year period, 118
    related or complementary activities, 117
    renewal, 117, 119–120
    rents, 118–119
    security of tenure, 116
    subletting, 118
    use or substitution of changed use, 117–118
  goodwill, of, 81–82
Leasing—
  financing company, 167–169
Legal issues—
  approach to, 9–11
Liability—
  banks, of, 173–174
  civil, 62–63

Liability—*contd*
  company, of—
    civil liability, 62–63
    criminal liability, 63
    credit establishments, of, 173–174
    criminal, 63
    directors, of, 63
    managers, of, 63
    members, of, 62
Libel—
  trade, 45
Licensing—
  industrial property, franchise as licence of, 107
  intellectual property, franchise as licence of, 107
  intuiti personnae, licence considered to be granted, 25
  know-how, 25
  obligatory licence, 26
  patents, 25
  trademarks, 25
Limited liability company—
  public—
    capital, 53–54
    English Plc, compared with, 52–53
    management, 54
    one tier system, 54–55
    two tier system, 55–56
  société anonyme. *See* public *above*
Limited partnership—
  nature of, 65
Litigation—
  pronuptia, 108
Loans—
  bank, from, 165–167
  société anonyme, finance for, 171–173

Management—
  insolvent business, of, 160–162
  SARL, of, 58–59
  société anonyme, of, 54
Managers—
  liability of, 63
Market sharing—
  prohibition on, 31
Maternity leave—
  entitlement, 135–136
Members—
  liability, 62
Merger—
  expert, appointment of, 73–74
  nature of, 71
  provisions governing, 71
  shareholders, meeting of, 74
  tax treatment, 75–77
  terms and conditions, 72–73
  valuation, 72
Model—
  procedure for registration, 22–23
  protection, 23–24
  registered, 21–22
  transfer, 23–24
  use, 23–24
Mortgage—
  real property, 113–114
Motor vehicle—
  exclusive distribution of, block exemption relating to, 33

Negotiable instruments—
  bills of exchange, 174–175
  cheques, 175–177
  Dailly's law, 178
  promissory notes, 177–178

Non-exclusive distributorship
  agreement—
  approved, 105
  selective, 104–105
Notary—
  essential function of, 7
  fees, 111
  sale and purchase, role relating to, 110
  transfer of undertaking, 73

Originating process
  court bailiff, served by, 4

Painter—
  statutory royalty, right to, 16
Partial asset transfer—
  nature of, 71
Partnership—
  civil company, 65–66
  general, 64
  limited, 65
  nature of, 64
  silent, 66
Passing-off—
  notion of, 44
Patents—
  licensing,
    agreement, block exemption relating to, 33
    form, 25–27
    generally, 25
    procedure, 25–27
  procedure, 12–13
  protection, 13–14
  revocation, 13–14

Personnel—
  enticing, 45
Planning—
  change of use, 188
  commercial use, 187–188
  environmental protection, 181–185
  land use plan, 188–189
  land uses, 187
Price fixing agreement—
  prohibition of, 31
Private company—
  share acquisitions, 82–85
Production—
  restrictions on, 31
Profits—
  corporate profit, meaning, 142–143
  employee profit sharing schemes, 134
Promissory notes—
  requirements relating to, 177–178
Pronuptia litigation—
  franchising, 108
Property, See Real property
Protection—
  copyright, relating to, 17–19
  design, of, 23–24
  environmental, See Environmental protection
  know-how, of, 21
  minority shareholders, of,
    case law, 61–62
    legal protection, 61
  model, of, 23–24
  patents, of, 13–14
  trademarks, of, 15–16

Public company—
  acquisition of—
    anti-trust provisions, 87–88
    bloc de contrôle, acquisition of, 86
    COB, 85–86
    generally, 85
    take-over bids, 86–87
Purchasing—
  commission agent, 95
  exclusive agreement, block exemption relating to, 32–33

Re-organisation—
  hive-off, *See* Hive-off
  merger, *See* Merger
Real property—
  generally, 109
  planning, 187–189
  sale and purchase—
    co-property interests, 110, 114–115
    completion, 112
    contract for sale of land, 110–111
    easements, 112–113
    expenses, 111–112
    fees, 111–112
    freehold interests, 110, 114–115
    incorporeal rights, 112–113
    mortgages, 113–114
    notary, transfer effected by, 110
    warranties, 113
  succession, 120–122
  types of transaction, 109
Registration tax—
  payment of, 50
  transactions subject to, 68–69

Rehabilitation proceedings—
  participants in—
    controleurs, 154
    court, 152
    employees' representatives, 154
    experts, 154
    insolvency practitioner, 153–154
    juge commissaire, 153
    public prosecutor, 153
  steps in—
    judgment period, 157–158
    liquidation, 158–159
    options in proceedings, 158–159
    rehabilitation period, 154–157
Relief—
  unfair competition, relating to, 46
Remedies—
  copyright, breach of, 17–19
Rent—
  business lease, 118–119
Research and development—
  agreement, block exemption relating to, 34–35
  restrictions on, 31
Revocation—
  patents, of, 13–14
  trademarks, of, 15–16
Royalty—
  painter's right to, 16
  sculptor's right to, 16

SARL, *See* Société à Responsabilité Limitée
Salary—
  employment contract, 127
Sale and purchase, *See* Real property

Sales—
  commission agent, 95
Sales representative
  functions, 98
  identity card, 98
  meaning, 98
Savoir faire, *See* Know-how
Scission, *See* Hive-off
Sculptor—
  statutory royalty, right to, 16
Secrets de fabrique, *See* Trade
  secrets
Security of tenure—
  business lease, 116
Self-employed—
  immigration, 124–125
  professional, 125
Shareholders—
  access to information, rights
    relating to, 61
  execution of statuts by, 50
  minority, protection of,
    61–62
  rights of—
    access to information, 61
    minority shareholders,
      protection of, 61–62
Shares—
  acquisition of, private company,
    82–85
  share options, 135
Silent partnership—
  nature of, 66
Social security system—
  contributions, 135
  employees, for, 135
Société, *See* Corporate body

Société à Responsabilité Limitée
  (SARL)—
  capital, 58
  management, 58–59
  number of members, 57
  societe anonyme, compared with,
    57–58
Société civile, *See* Civil company
Sole trader—
  formalities on commencement, 67
  goodwill, 67–68
  nature of, 47
  status of, 66
Sources of law—
  principal, 1
Specialisation agreement—
  block exemption, 34
Stock Exchange Commission—
  role of, 85–86
  take-over bids, 86–87
Succession—
  real property, 120–122
Superior court—
  non-commercial cases heard by, 4
  patent, revocation of, 14
Supervisory Board—
  société anonyme, 56
Supply contract—
  rules governing, 104
Supreme Court—
  court of appeal, appeal from, 4

Take-over bid—
  organisations involved, 86–87
  rules and regulations, 87
Taxation—
  accounts, 137

Index

Taxation—*contd*
  business—
    direct, 138–139
    indirect, 141–142
    tax incentives, 139–141
  corporate profit, meaning, 142–143
  corporation tax, 68
  direct personal tax, 143–145
  hive-off, treatment of, 75–77
  investigation, 137
  merger, treatment of, 75–77
  personal income tax, 68
  registration tax, 68–69, 143–144
  transfer pricing, 145–146
  value added tax, 137–138
Third party—
  employment contract, 127
Tie-in agreement—
  prohibition of, 31
Trade—
  libel, 45
  Member States, between, 30
Trade secrets—
  meaning, 20–21
  misuse of, 45
  procedure, 19–21
Trade union—
  worker representation through, 133
Trademarks—
  licensing—
    form, 25–27
    generally, 25
    procedure, 25–27
    procedure, 14–15

Trademarks—*contd*
  licensing—*contd*
    protection, 15–16
    revocation, 15–16
Transfer pricing—
  taxation, 145–166
Transparancy—
  competition law and, 42–43
Tribunal de commerce, *See* Companies Registry

Undertakings—
  collusion between, prohibition relating to, 28–29
Unfair competition—
  enticing personnel, 45
  generally, 43–44
  passing-off, 44
  relief, 46
  slander of goods, 45
  trade libel, 45
  trade secrets, misuse of, 45–46
  unfair advertising, 44

Value added tax—
  ambit of, 137–138
  exemptions, 138
  property, 138
  standard rate, 138
Voyageur représentant placier, *See* Sales representative

Waste—
  control of, 185–186
Winding-up—
  insolvency, measures intended to prevent, 151